THE NATURE OF MAN
ACCORDING TO THE VEDANTA

First Sentient Publications edition, 2004

Cover and book design by Nicholas Cummings

Library of Congress Cataloging-in-Publication Data

Levy, John, 1910-1976.
   The nature of man according to the Vedanta / by John Levy.~ 1st
Sentient Publications ed.
      p. cm.
   ISBN 1-59181-024-8
   1. Vedanta. 2. Self (Philosophy) 3. Man (Hinduism) I. Title.
B132.V3L4 2004 128~dc22

                                                    2004011181

Printed in the United States of America

10 9 8 7 6 5 4 3 2

SENTIENT PUBLICATIONS

A Limited Liability Company
1113 Spruce St.
Boulder, CO 80302
www.sentientpublications.com

THE NATURE OF MAN ACCORDING TO THE VEDANTA

John Levy

SENTIENT PUBLICATIONS, LLC

Also by John Levy

IMMEDIATE KNOWLEDGE AND HAPPINESS (SADY-MUKTI)

Contents

Preface   1

Part One: The Distinction of Standpoints   13

I. Introductory Chapter   14
To Whom Is This Method of Inquiry Addressed?   14
The Desire for Happiness   14
The Three States of Man   15

II. Waking and Dreaming   17
The Waking-State   17
The Dream-State   17
A First Comparison of Waking and Dreaming   17
A Comparison of Thinking and Dreaming   18
The Equivalence of Thinking and Dreaming   19
A Further Comparison of Waking and Dreaming   19
The Need to Define Objective Experience   20
Duality   20

III. Dreamless Sleep and the Real Self   21
Dreamless Sleep   21
Sleeping Experience   21
The Singleness of Non-Mental Experience   22
An Objection   23
The Objection Refuted   23
Reductio ad Absurdum   24
The Interval between Two Thoughts   24
Other States that Are Identical with Sleep   25
Summary of Part One   25

Part Two: Objective Experience   27

IV. Introduction to the Analysis of Objective Experience   28
   Objective Experience   28
   The Two Kinds of Cognition   28
   A Thought Is Not an Entity   29
   Abstract Thought and Generalization   29
   The Objects of Consciousness   29
   Sensory Perception   30

V. Sensory Perception and the Notion of Objects   31
   How the Notion of an Object Arises   31
   The Correlation of Sense-Objects and the Senses   31
   The Oneness of the Perceiver and the Perceived   32
   The Relation between Brain, Sense-Organs and the
     Outer World   33
   How the Notion of a World Arises   34
   Conclusion: Sensations as the Words of a Sensory Language   35
   Postscript: A Word about Intuition   35

VI. The Body and the Sensory Faculty   37
   The Body and Its World   37
   One's Body an Object of Consciousness   37
   One's Body a Notion   37

VII. The Sensory Nature of the World   38
   The Relation between the Percipient's Body and
     Foreign Bodies   38
   The Notion of Other Persons' Bodies   38

VIII. Common Sense and the Testimony of Others   40
   The Limitations of Common Sense   40
   The Attribution of Life to Other Bodies   41
   Conclusion: A Means to Rising above the
     Commonsense Outlook   41

IX. The Unreal Dualism of Mind and Matter 43
 No Distinction between the Mental and the Physical 43
 Insoluble Problems 43

X. Two Common Misunderstandings 45
 Bishop Berkeley, Bertrand Russell, and Dr. Samuel Johnson 45

XI. The Illusion of Materiality 47
 Materiality 47
 Length and Breadth 47
 Depth 48
 The Physiological Aspect of Tridimensionality 48
 Continuity 49
 The Psychological Origin of Tridimensionality 50
 The Aim of This Analysis 51
 Summary 51

XII. Space 52
 The Concept of Space and the Illusion of Materiality 52
 Distance and Proximity 52
 Conclusion 54

XIII. The Illusions of Causality 55
 Change 55
 Cause and Effect 55
 Relationship 56
 Summary: The Illusion of Relationship 56

XIV. Time and Space 57
 The Relation of Space to Time 57
 The Concept of Time 57

XV. Time and Timelessness 59
 Duration and the Notion of Time 59
 Time 60

The Passage of Time and Pure Being   60

The Apprehension of Timelessness   60

XVI. Time and the Present Eternity   62

The Situating of Experience in Time   62

Past, Present and Future   63

Sleep and Non-Duality   63

Time and the Present Eternity   64

Conclusion: The Ego and Non-Duality   64

Part Three: The Self   67

XVII. The Definition of a Human Being   68

Individuality and Personality   68

The Self   68

Personal Identity   68

The Immutable Self   69

The Definition of a Human Being   69

XVIII. Identification   70

The Personal Pronoun and Identification   70

The Personal Pronoun and Unconsciousness   70

The Personal Pronoun and Consciousness   71

XIX. Consciousness and Mental Activity   72

The Different Aspects of Thought   72

Mental Activity Defined   72

Thought   72

The Thinker   73

Conclusion   74

XX. The Illusion of Duality   75

Duality Defined   75

Subject and Object   75

Memory and Ignorance   76

XXI. Life, Memory and Desire   77

XXII. The Origin of Memory, and the Witness   78
    The Thinker an Object of Consciousness   78
    Egoism and the Act of Remembering   78
    Memory and Identification   78
    Memory and the Witness   79
    The Twofold Nature of the Ego, and the Witness   79

XXIII. The Dissolution of Egoism and the Restitution of the Self   81
    The Ego and the Non-Dual Self   81
    The Restitution of the Self   82
    The Gist of the Method   82
    The Superiority of This Method   83
    An Injunction Regarding the Personal Application
       of the Method   84

XXIV. The Verbal Expression of Non-Duality   85

XXV. The Problem of Relation   86
    Consciousness and the Brain   86
    The Brain as the Locus of Objective Experience   87
    No Direct Interrelation of Percepts   87
    The Problem   88
    The Dissolution of the Problem   88

XXVI. Non-Duality   90
    The Disparity of Consciousness and Objects   90
    The Inadequacy of the Written Word and
       Metaphysical Realization   90
    Direct Knowledge   92
    On Expressing the Inexpressible   92
    The Seer and the Seen   93
    Non-Duality   93

Matter, Mind and Non-Duality   94
Wave and Water   96

XXVII. Metaphysical Realization and the Non-Existence of Memory 97
Metaphysical Realization   97
Succession Never Experienced   97
The Non-Existence of Memory   98

XXVIII. Absurd Questions   100
The Origin of the World   100
The Origin of Identification   100
The Fundamental Problem   101
Absurd Prospects   101

Part Four: Self-Love   103

XXIX. Desires, Feelings, and the Witness   104
The Objects of Desire   104
Peace the Ultimate Object of Every Desire   104
The Process of Enjoyment   105
The Analysis of Feeling   105
Feelings and the Witness   106
Realization and Renunciation   106
Conclusion: The Yearning for Happiness   107

XXX. Self-Love   109
Self-Love the Spring of All Actions   109
On Helping Others   110

Preface

A Life in Retrospect

It was in Paris that my real education began.[1] I was nineteen when I went there to be a draughtsman-apprentice to the architect Auguste Perret. He received me in person and at first I was rather awed by his presence, with his bearded dignity, his proud stance to which high heels discreetly lent support, and his manner of speaking like an oracle, full of the consciousness of his achievement. He was, in fact, one of the foremost architects of his time and the first, I believe, to make use of reinforced concrete logically and unashamedly, some will say for good and others for bad. At all events, logic and audacity are in themselves qualities to be admired, and he did much to rid the world of nineteenth-century sham: for that, all lovers of honest building must be grateful. Monsieur Auguste, as we called him, used to sit in his chair facing a photograph of the Parthenon. The remarkable thing was that every design which bore his name could not have come from any other source, although he was never seen to make a single drawing and he left all the details to be worked out by draftsmen, many of whom, like myself, were young men from foreign countries who thought it an honor to be able to work under his direction.

---

1. It is uncommon to find an impersonal treatise prefaced by an introduction where the author himself, in the most personal manner, recalls how he was led to the position from which his work derives. When the publishers first proposed it, the idea struck the writer of this work as being quite inapt. But when, further, they strongly urged that its incorporation* could be of help to those who at present are not engaged in this or in any similar approach to metaphysical realization, to those, in other words, who might wrongly feel themselves to be outsiders, he could not but acquiesce.

* This appeared as an article in the *Hibbert Journal*, January 1954.

Moreover, since he was his own contractor and employed his own engineers, one had the unique experience of making the architectural designs, the structural drawings and of supervising the work in progress on the building-yards, a combination of aesthetics, theory, mathematics and the purely practical which gave me my first real insight into the underlying unity of all things. That is why I said my real education began in Paris.

My interest in architecture was not such, however, as to make me wish to devote my life to it, and I turned to the study of music, the art with which I have the greatest natural affinity and which has always attracted me more than any other. Like architecture, music is also an art of construction; but being fluid, so to speak, it is a better vehicle for the expression of emotion and intuition. Whilst the time I spent with Perret was a period of intellectual awakening and discipline, the years I spent with the gifted Nadia Boulanger helped me to unite the head and the heart, a movement that almost everyone in our time has to accomplish, since these two are often so tragically divorced.

Amongst the musicians and artists I used to meet, the question of originality was frequently discussed. I began to see that in order to be truly original, one must first go to the very origin of things. It was becoming clear to me that what I was seeking was not a *means* of expression, but the *background of experience* that thoughts and feelings can only inadequately express. All this came home to me when I compared our discordant modern civilization with the more natural order of the old. Most thinking people have made the same comparison, and it was obvious that the splendid products of traditional civilizations, such as the medieval, were intimately connected with spiritual conviction. I wondered how one might recapture this feeling. Empty as much of our modern life is, it is not, certainly, wholly negative. And its more positive qualities and attitudes in which I believed seemed to deny the beliefs and the attitudes of civilizations which had their foundations in religion and tradition. Though I did later adopt the forms of religious orthodoxy for a specific purpose, I began at first to look for traces of the truth they expressed as distinct from its expression in ritual and dogma. It is unfortunate that most people tend to dismiss the whole spiritual domain simply because they see only its unhappier manifestations in degenerated organized religion. I felt like the Jew in the Decameron, who was converted to Christianity after a visit to Rome where he saw nothing but corruption, and decided that a Church whose spiritual life was so intense, in spite of this depravity at its very centre, must represent a truth far beyond human frailty. I felt that all the great manifestations of religious conviction, such as a Romanesque church or Catholic Mass, pointed to an attainable end. Seeing no reason why I should not also acquire such a certitude, I set about seeking knowledge.

I began to study medieval music, and especially the music of Guillaume de Machaut, for he seemed to be more consciously concerned than his successors with metaphysics. I looked into the symbolism of ancient art and poetry. I also began reading a great many books in the hope of discovering the truth, whatever it might be. I read Greek philosophy in all its variety and found it to be quite unrelated to any present practical possibilities. Occultism and theosophy, both products of our time, while expressing a certain aspiration, lapsed in the end into wistful obscurity, when not into intellectual snobbery; as did also the many other untraditional schools of thought with which the world abounds. I read the works of Ouspensky and was taken to see him: though his writings helped me then, I found later that he only travestied some quite genuine teachings and methods of the East. And then, at last, I was introduced to the writings of René Guénon. I owe to Guénon the sudden understanding that I and the universe are one and that this essential unity can actually be realized. Now I find much to criticize in his attitude: and, in particular, his statement of Vedanta is often misleading. But his writings opened my eyes then and gave me a foretaste of the truth. His expression, "the Supreme Identity," by which he referred to this essential oneness of the individual soul and the universal soul, struck the deepest chord in my being.

It was this and one other thing that really gave me my direction. That other thing was the need of finding a competent personal guidance, without which absolute knowledge cannot be attained. All virile spiritual traditions have proclaimed this necessity. It is no mere formality nor, as some people think, is it an evasion of one's own responsibility. Lasting spiritual realization of the highest degree has never been observed to come by itself, and cannot in fact do so, because so long as a man believes himself to be a limited individual, the reality which is his essential being will lie hidden. The seeker must therefore be enabled to realize that his essential self, far from being what his individualistic habits of thought would make it seem, is beyond limitation and thus infinite and eternal. Only one who has himself fully realized this can enable another to realize it. Although it was not until I came into contact with a true sage that I could define a spiritual master's function, I had at once an intuitive sense of what it implied, just as I had of what Guénon called the Supreme Identity. From that time onward, the aim of all the different steps I took was to find such a guidance, and I now know that true guidance is synonymous with true knowledge.

My first step was to adopt orthodox Judaism. Let me explain. One of Guénon's most specious ideas was the theory of the fundamental oneness of all orthodox spiritual or religious traditions. He is not alone in this: it has become the fashion. And I notice that Aldous Huxley, for instance, can hardly bring himself to mention one tradition without feeling obliged to add a list of several others. Anyway, Guénon's theory put every tradition on an equal footing, if not in its present state of survival, at least at its origin. It is important to understand how this over-generous assumption took root in his mind. From the very beginning of his devotion to metaphysics, the Hindu doctrine of Non-Duality or Adwaita had given him his standard of truth. This is not surprising, for there only is the truth unambiguously expressed without its being embroiled in a mass of historical and other irrelevancies. With the bird's-eye view it gives to whomsoever has been able to grasp its implications, one can hardly avoid the tendency to discover, in the statements of the prophets, the saints and the scriptures, revelations of the highest truth, when possibly these statements indicate nothing but a deep intuition; and to see, in the whole paraphernalia of religious art and ritual, conscious symbols of the ultimate reality, when they only show a leaning towards it. There is, moreover, a constant temptation to look for points of comparison between different spiritual doctrines. All this takes one away from the truth itself. At the time, however, I was charmed to find a theory which seemed in a moment to reconcile all differences. Taking it to the letter, I thought that the proper and adequate course to adopt was to return to the religion of my fathers, though I had been brought up liberally in the English public-school tradition, and had passed most of my life as an agnostic. In short, I became an orthodox Jew.

I did so with all my heart, attaching myself to a Rabbinical school, scrupulously following every orthodox precept and enjoying daily conversation with the head of the college, a cheerful and learned man who was descended from a line of Cabbalistic Rabbis. He had been born and brought up in Jerusalem, and was steeped in the atmosphere of this essential Judaism, commonly so misunderstood by Jews and non-Jews alike. Cabbala means literally tradition: it is the oral transmission of the deep understanding, said to come down directly from Moses, David, Solomon and other prophets. Such knowledge cannot be conveyed by the bare statements of the scriptures. I hoped, by adopting Judaism, that I would find a master in this Cabbala.

With the background acquired from the study of Guénon's writings and, if I may say so, as a result of my own earnest endeavors, the time I spent in this path was anything but a dissipation. It helped me to convert into a single stream the disordered currents of my aspirations. And for the first time in my life I felt myself to be anchored to a changeless principle that I could not as yet fully discern. This may astonish those accustomed to take their knowledge from books. But spiritual knowledge is not theoretical: either it is immediate or else it is no knowledge at all. You can talk to an Eskimo about life in the tropics, but he cannot, without living there, really know what it is.

I learnt many things; and one great intellectual difficulty was partially resolved. I refer to the notion that the universe was created out of nothing by the will of God. As the complete resolution of this difficulty at the end of my search was also largely the means by which I attained certitude, I shall allow myself to expatiate upon it. The notion implies that a self-sufficient, infinite and eternal Principle has desires, an absurdity that no thinking man can honestly admit. And yet, unless he had desires, how could the Supreme Being determine to create a universe? If the universe is a creation, it means that the creator as such is not infinite, for the infinite and the finite cannot together exist.

A close study of the Hebrew text of the Genesis, in the light of Cabbalistic commentaries and with the explanations of my Rabbi, showed me that although the literal meaning is as usually understood, the real meaning goes much deeper. It is not possible for me now to enter upon a word-for-word explanation of the text, but I can say that there is no suggestion of the world being created out of nothing, or that its creator was God in his highest aspect. This is quite in accordance with the cosmological explanation openly propounded by the lower Vedanta, namely, that the world is an idea in the mind of a personal and conditioned Deity, who has his periods of waking and sleeping, on the analogy of human experience: quite logically so, since he is said to have created man in his own image: and what applies to the one must apply to the other. In the periods of his sleeping, the world-idea enters into latency and ceases to be manifest: it becomes manifest when this conditioned Deity awakens. The physical world as such is therefore nothing but an idea and has no existence apart from its being thought of. Bishop Berkeley expressed the same thing in another way in his famous enunciation that the being of all objects is to be perceived or known. In his zeal to prove the existence of God, however, Berkeley appears to have overlooked the fact that any conception one may form of God as a principle distinct from oneself also comes within the category of objects perceived. It follows from this that the very being of an objectively conceived God is also to be perceived or known. Vedanta, at a higher level, has to face the same problem. It concludes that God as such is not the ultimate reality.

Ultimate reality: these words can hardly mean anything. The ultimate reality, whatever it is, cannot be worded, nor can it be rationalized. What these words express is usually only a hunger which concepts and predicates, even creeds, entirely fail to meet, a hunger that is innate in every enquiring person.

What then is the solution? For my own part I have found it in Non-Dualistic Vedanta, an ancient and evergreen tradition that thrives even today. The approach is subjective and is founded upon an analysis of one's own experience, which is that I-myself, not as an embodied being but as the conscious principle which is the basis of all my experience and all my knowledge, I-myself, then, am the sole principle I can know certainly to exist: this knowledge is immediate in all men and it requires no proving. As Shankaracharya, who lived in about 800 A.D. and is the best known exponent of Adwaita (Non-Duality), says,

> Whoever doubts the fact that he himself exists? If you do doubt it, it is still you yourself who doubt it. It is a matter of direct experience that the I is devoid of change, whereas the body is incessantly changing. How then can the body be the self? All persons carry on their respective activities by means of the sense of I-ness or selfhood and the sense of this-ness or objectivity. Of these, the former relates to the inner self and the latter to external objects [like the body, the senses and the mind]. Having understood the meaning of the word, I, to be the pure, transcendental, secondless self that is different from the body, the senses and other objects, no other meaning should be attributed to it. By mistaking the self to be the individual soul, just as, in the dark, a rope is mistaken for a serpent, a man is subject to fear. When he realizes "I am not the individual soul but the supreme self," then he is free from fear. Although the self, being of the nature of consciousness, cannot therefore be the object of consciousness, there can never be a doubt regarding the absolute existence of consciousness itself.

Shankaracharya also describes the state of a man who has risen above fear because he has ceased to identify himself with the body, and this again because he has realized his self as the consciousness in which the ideas of incarnation and objectivity spring up.

Birth, old age, decay and death are of no concern to me, for I am not the body. The world of sound, touch, sight, taste and smell has no connection with me, for I am not the senses. I am not the mind and therefore sorrow, desire, hatred and fear cannot affect me. As declared by the scripture, the self is neither the senses nor the mind: it is unconditioned.

And in a rather different language, the *Bhagavad-Gita*, perhaps the most venerated book in India, gives the following description of a self-realized man.

When a man has found delight and satisfaction and peace in his true self, then he is no longer obliged to perform any kind of action. He has nothing to gain in this world by action, and nothing to lose by refraining from action. He is independent of everybody and everything.

This is, of course, because he no longer identifies himself with his body, which alone acts and which alone can gain or lose. But a literal interpretation might cause people to renounce their activities and their duties. The *Gita* therefore says, "Do your duty, always . . . without anxiety about results." This certainly seems to me to be the only solution: it is exactly the one that we are all blindly seeking in a world where freedom, independence and peace are on everyone's lips. Not very practical, I can almost hear you saying! But I should say that this is the only practical way of attaining real peace and independence. It can never be found in terms of a body that is entirely dependent upon circumstances. As the *Gita* says, "All mankind is born for perfection, and each shall attain it, will he but follow his nature's duty." In this connection, I am reminded of the answer given by a sage to someone who asked him why he did not go out into the world and preach this truth to all men. "You can cover the earth with leather," he replied, "or you can wear your own shoes."

I have now given some idea of the final position, and there is little purpose in my speaking at length of the several years during which, still in search of genuine guidance, and having adopted the religion of Mohammed, I lived as a Muslim, practiced the rites of orthodox Islam and performed the disciplines, the ritual dances and the meditations of an Order of Sufis, under the direction of a Sheikh. I should explain that what Cabbala is to Judaism, Sufism is to Islam. Now, the characteristic of *all* religions on the level at which they serve the needs of ordinary men is the acceptance of the duality of God and man, though usually there is in their scriptures something that points to a higher truth. In the Old Testament, for example, we repeatedly find the expression, "I am the Lord Thy God"; and in the New, there is the statement of Jesus, "The Kingdom of Heaven is within you." Similar pointers are not wholly lacking in the Quran and are to be found especially in the recorded sayings of the Prophet. Great Sufis like Muhyuddin Ibn Arabi have rightly given them a metaphysical interpretation, although they seldom if ever give arguments to show why the reality is necessarily subjective, a thing Vedantins invariably do, the better to help aspirants to overcome the individualistic habits of thought of which I have previously spoken. But the unseeking Muslim, like the unseeking Jew or Christian, unfortunately has always been firmly wedded to dualism and has often sought to destroy anyone who, having transcended it, has been so bold as to proclaim the fact. The example of Mansur, who was beheaded for declaring, "Ana'l-Haqq—I am the truth," is evidence enough. Al-Haqq, which means literally the truth, is one of the ninety-nine names of Allah, so to a Muslim, "Ana'l-Haqq" means "I am Allah": this is considered to be the most dreadful blasphemy

10

a man can utter. One may suppose that the possibility of its being true was almost totally ignored. Of course, a man as such cannot be God as such, but the essential reality of God, as distinct from what mankind ascribes to him, cannot be different from the essential reality of a man who has realized his self as that which is beyond all human attributes.

Duality colors the mind of all who are brought up with the Quran as their scripture, and the result of this limitation is that Sufism, which has lost its force and is moribund, at present can offer only a path based on devotion and not upon knowledge, which, if the ultimate reality is to be found, is the necessary complement to the other. It is in many ways parallel to the dualists of India who say they only want to taste the sugar, which stands for the truth, and not to become it. Whereas the very basis of Non-Dualistic Vedanta is that it is impossible to become something you are not already: you have only to become aware of what you actually are, that is to say, absolute consciousness or knowledge when self is viewed from the standpoint of thought, absolute bliss or peace from the standpoint of feelings, and absolute existence from the standpoint of life. Even so, this awareness is not considered by Vedantins to be enough: it is one thing to have recognized your essential being, but what of the world? In Islam, just as there is no real analysis of the self, there is practically none of the world in terms of sensory perception, which in reality constitutes it, as already indicated when I spoke of Berkeley and in the lines of Shankaracharya. In Non-Dualistic Vedanta, this analysis is considered to be quite essential: without it, your experience of the world remains unexplained and complete knowledge is then impossible.

Let it not be thought that I wish to disparage the admirable religion of Islam, for what I have said about its limitations applies equally to all other religions as such. In spite of these deficiencies at the highest level, Islam gave me the most invaluable help and brought me to the state of heart and mind in which I could receive the pure truth from a great Vedantin. That was in India, several years ago, and my life really began at that moment. Needless to say, because I have passed through so many phases to arrive at a solution, it does not follow that others have to do the same. Perhaps, from one angle, it was necessary that I should have had to pursue such a roundabout path in order the better to assure my fellow-seekers that the truth, in the end, is utterly simple and self-evident. As Shankaracharya says,

> The self that is ever-present in all beings appears, through a misconception, to be unattained. But when this wrong knowledge has been destroyed by true knowledge, it is seen always to have been attained, just as after searching everywhere for a necklace, the seeker finds it around his neck.

The verses from the *Bhagavad-Gita* are taken from the translation of Swami Prabhavananda and Christopher Isherwood, published by Phoenix House, London.

The quotations from Shankaracharya are culled and adopted by the author from the several treatises given in the *Select Works of Sri S.*, published by G. A. Natesan and Co., Madras.

PART ONE

THE DISTINCTION OF STANDPOINTS

WAKING, DREAMING, AND DREAMLESS SLEEP

–I–

Introductory Chapter

To Whom Is This Method of Inquiry Addressed?

The difficulties are immense in writing a book of this nature. Most Hindus have done it in the form of aphoristic verse, easy to memorize but needing interpretation in accordance with the living tradition. That in fact the reader had grown up in it and so would be on intimate terms with the subject they could take for granted until quite recently, when the printing of Vedantic works, and their publication in foreign tongues, at once did away with the old guarantees. As a result, it would be perilous now to presuppose any real familiarity even on the part of serious students, whether Indian or not; and therefore in writing this book, my only assumption has been that its readers seek knowledge of the ultimate truth; and as a rider, that they come with an open mind and the capacity to go beyond the written word. To such kindred souls I address the pages that follow. Therein I have endeavored to give a clear account of the highest Vedanta, known as Adwaita (Non-Duality), without stooping to make any of those compromises attendant upon the childish desire to convert others.

The Desire for Happiness

It cannot be disputed that happiness is the sole aim in life, yet most men would find it hard to agree to this statement without some reservation. What is the fundamental cause of their embarrassment? Is it not that life ends in death and that the prospect of death teems with incertitude? Not all men, of course, care to think seriously of death, but all men, in normal circumstances, run spontaneously from danger, unless to risk it is their duty or their pleasure. In that case, they have ceased for the moment to identify themselves with the body; and this is what happens to all of us in moments of happiness. Now if we can transcend this false identification unwittingly, can we not do so knowingly? It is the purpose of this book to show that we can, not only from time to time but once and for all. Indeed, we are always and by nature other than the body, for while the body changes continually from birth to death, we who seem to be one with it can observe and remember its modifications. It follows that if, instead of our claiming to be a changeful personality, we could regain our true centre, that immutable, conscious self which observes the personality, we should at once and for ever be happy and peaceful, because we would then know for certain that what affected the body could not affect our self. This, in short, will be the conclusion of our Inquiry.

The Three States of Man

To find a peace and happiness that is beyond every possible circumstance including death, we must be in a position to discern the changeless principle within us. This will entail an examination of human experience as a whole. As human beings, we experience three states, those of waking, dreaming and dreamless sleep, in which all our experience is comprised. But it will not be enough to consider these states from the sole standpoint of waking, as we normally do, for little can be learnt about a whole from the limited standpoint of one of its parts. Accordingly, we shall consider each state from different points of view: from its own, from that which is common to waking and dreaming, and from the one that transcends every state as such. The latter is the standpoint of the real self in man, the self which continues unmodified throughout the three states, from birth to death, and indeed, beyond birth and death.

–II–

Waking and Dreaming

The Waking-State

The waking-state is commonly held to consist of thinking and feeling in the presence of tangible objects. Tangible objects are perceived through the five organs of sensory perception. These organs we shall call collectively the bodily senses.

The Dream-State

The dream-state, from the standpoint of the waking, consists only of thinking and feeling. But the dreamer has no idea that he is dreaming, for according to his experience, tangible objects are also perceived. Thus the dream-state is definable in exactly the same terms as the waking.

A First Comparison of Waking and Dreaming

When we compare the two states, each being viewed from its own standpoint, no difference can be found. A difference appears, however, when we consider dreams from the standpoint of waking, according to which waking alone is a real experience. On waking, we know that the dream-world, together with the dream-body whose senses perceived it, were products of the mind. The question then arises whether the waking-man's thoughts and the dreamer's whole experience are not equivalent.

A Comparison of Thinking and Dreaming

Thinking is supposed to differ from dreaming on several scores, notwithstanding our knowledge that both are mental. Let us look at some of these alleged differences:

(a) First, dreams are said to derive, and not to be distinct, from waking experience. If so, this would apply equally to the thoughts that occur in the waking-state.

(b) Second, some dreams are said to derive from a latent store of impressions which contemporary psychology calls the subconscious mind. Granting the existence of a subconscious mind, so do some thoughts.[1]

(c) Third, the dream-body and the dream-mind are said to do or think things the waking-body and the waking-mind cannot. This is true in respect of bodies but not in respect of thoughts. I can imagine, as I may dream, that my body is flying. I can imagine that I meet and talk with the dead or with people unknown to me in my waking experience; and that these are events in this or in other worlds and in this or in other eras, just as I may dream that they are. Moreover, I can imagine, as I may dream, that my body is in another condition of health and age, or that my mind is differently disposed in one way or another.

(d) Fourth, while thinking in the waking-state may appear at times to be deliberate and at others involuntary, dreaming, from the waker's standpoint, must always appear to be involuntary. This is a confusion, for if the dream-state is entered involuntarily, so is the waking-state. But in dreaming as well as in waking, we may seem to choose our thoughts.

---

1. From the standpoint of consciousness, what is not now its object does not now exist. This will be made clear in due course; and then the expression, "subconscious mind," could only be regarded as a contradiction in terms.

(e) Fifth, it is supposed that events occurring in dreams would occupy less time than similar events if they occurred in waking experience. This is to equate the standard of time in our perception of tangible objects to that in our thinking about them when there are, in fact, two different standards. We require no more time to think of any particular event in the waking state than we do to dream of it. But if we can thus divide the waking-state into thinking and the perception of tangible objects, we must apply the same distinction to the dream-state, for to the dreaming subject, his experience is also one of waking, divisible in the same manner, with two distinct standards of time. Thus, there is no necessary variance between thinking and dreaming as regards our experience of time.

The Equivalence of Thinking and Dreaming

These considerations have helped to establish the equivalence of thinking and dreaming: both are states of mental activity. If any difference in detail can be discovered, it is no more than the difference between one mode of thought and another.

A Further Comparison of Waking and Dreaming

We have seen that thinking, feeling and the perception of tangible objects are activities common both to waking and dreaming experience, each being viewed from its own standpoint. But on entering the waking-state, a dream is found to have been a mental product in every one of its aspects; and yet to the dreamer the so-called dream-state was one of waking. What reasons have we to suppose that the present waking-state is anything but a mental product, just like a dream? In the second part of this work, we shall come to see that tangible objects have no independent existence. They exist as notions in the perceiver's mind; and thus between mind and matter the distinction is unreal, as it is also between the thought and the perception of a tangible object. If this be granted, then to be awake has no meaning and there is no waking-state: it is all a dream. But a dream, so called only from the standpoint of an inexistent waking-state, is also a misnomer.

The Need to Define Objective Experience

We are now looking at dreaming and waking from the vantage point of the single, immutable, and conscious self which pervades and illuminates all our objective experience. There being no essential difference between one state of objective experience and another, a term that serves equally to describe all states in which the mind is active must be found.

Duality

Waking and dreaming are states of mental activity, whose characteristic is the presence of a knower and a known, or a thinker and a thought, the one being conscious of the other. Mental activity is therefore to be defined as the state of duality, the duality of subject and object.

Dreamless Sleep and the Real Self

Dreamless Sleep

Dreamless sleep may best be defined as that state in which the seeming duality of subject and object has disappeared. Its negative characteristic is the absence of mental activity, a term I use to include thinking, feeling, and sensory perception. From its own standpoint, however, dreamless sleep must be positive, for we cannot experience mere negation: and then the absence of mental activity is not its true characteristic. It follows that when we talk of dreamless sleep, of the absence of mental activity, and say upon waking that we slept soundly and knew nothing, we are viewing it solely from the standpoint of duality, by comparison with which sleep is a state of nescience.[1] It follows, moreover, that none of the positive terms we apply to our waking and dreaming experience can be applied literally to our experience of sleeping. There are, nevertheless, three positive aspects of sleep, the knowledge of which will enable us to recognize its true nature.

Sleeping Experience

(a) The first appears plainly from the fact that we do not cease to exist when asleep, though all objective, individual

---

1. The following illustration from everyday life will afford a useful comparison. Suppose I place a pen in the palm of my hand and ask someone to tell me what he sees. He will answer that he sees a pen. Suppose now that I put the pen down and again ask him what he sees. In nine cases out of ten, he will answer, "Nothing," when in fact he sees the palm of my hand.

experience has vanished. It must be this: profound sleep, in itself, is the state of unconditioned being. I mean that in dreamless sleep there remains a principle transcending qualities or accidents, these pertaining to objectivity.

(b) The second follows from the fact that on waking we are conscious of having slept soundly, though absence as such can never be experienced. It must be this: profound sleep, in itself, is the state of non-duality. I mean that the principle of consciousness remains without its seeming to assume the duality of a conscious subject and its object.

(c) The third is proven by the confidence with which we look forward to the enjoyment associated with sound sleep; and also by the feeling of an actual deprivation when we suffer from insomnia. It must be this: profound sleep, from its own standpoint, is the state of self-contentment. I mean that when desire and the objects of desire have vanished with the cessation of mental activity, what remains is the positive import of desirelessness.

The Singleness of Non-Mental Experience

Unconditioned being, non-dual consciousness, and perfect peace, these three characteristics of profound sleep correspond to the three constituents of individual experience, namely, life, thought and feeling. But they are no more than aspects of the real self which must be single and immutable, single because it observes, and therefore transcends, the variety of objective experience, whenever the latter arises; and immutable because it remains unaffected by the appearance or the non-appearance of that variety. We could not, however, know anything about it if we departed from our unconditioned state on seeming to enter the objective domain. It follows that non-duality continues as the background of duality.

Not until we approach the end of this work will all the implications of the present paragraph have been appreciated.

An Objection

An objection to our describing one aspect of sleep as the state of unconditioned being is likely to be raised. It is that the mind, though in abeyance, cannot be wholly absent, for otherwise a sleeper could not be roused by sensations.

The Objection Refuted

The objection implies that what we view as dreamless sleep from the standpoint of duality is the experience of a sleeper, that the subject of the subject-object relationship remains, in fact, even when there is no objectivity. It assumes, moreover, that the waking-body persists in sleep. But do others not see it? Now other bodies, like our own, are notions that belong to the particular state of mental activity at present being experienced. If others observe some response to a stimulus in what they see as a sleeper's body or brain, they do so as a part of their waking experience and they tell us so as a part of ours. But when we are having no objective experience, there are no bodies and therefore no others. The objection is therefore illogical: what seemed to be a problem is merely a confusion of standpoints. From the standpoint of duality, experience must always seem to be personal and thus to be connected with someone's body; but from that of non-duality, there is no personality and consequently no sleeper and no sleeping-body. The objection is refuted.

Reductio ad Absurdum

Moreover, even if for argument's sake we admitted the latent existence of thought and the continued manifestation of a waking-body in profound sleep, the fact remains that in order to be conscious of sensations affecting the waking-body, we must already be awake.[2]

The Interval between Two Thoughts

Mental action is not continuous. Each thought, feeling or sensory perception has a beginning and an end. It follows that between one conscious mentation and another there is an interval. From the dualistic point of view, the interval will appear to be infinitesimally brief. But in itself, it transcends the notion of time, time being experienced only when there is mental activity. Here there is none and so it normally escapes our attention. If we try to think of it, it will appear as a state of nescience.

Now this periodic suspension of mental activity is identical with dreamless sleep, which we thus experience at every other moment, so to say, in the midst of waking and dreaming experience. I have stated in another connection (The Singleness of Non-Mental Experience) that non-duality continues as the background of duality. It may be compared to the paper on which these words are printed.

---

2. In this connection, let me observe that dreamless sleep is of short duration relative to the whole period of rest. It lasts normally from one to three hours; in the remaining period, objectivity is often present in one form or another. It should go without saying that this reference to the duration of dreamless sleep is valid only from the empirical standpoint: it has no meaning from the metaphysical, as we shall see in the section that follows.

Other States that Are Identical with Sleep

Fainting-fits, catalepsy, total anesthesia, trances in which thought subsides,[3] and the sort of absent-mindedness of which, when asked what thoughts we are having, we can only say, "I wasn't thinking of anything," are similarly characterized by the absence of duality. All these are identical with profound sleep and the interval between two thoughts. Any apparent difference pertains solely to the state of mind which preceded or followed them.

Summary of Part One

As human beings, we experience three states, waking, dreaming and dreamless sleep. The first two are states of mental activity, characterized by the duality of a conscious subject and its object. The third is a state of non-duality, characterized by the absence of objective experience and the continued presence of the real self, which may be described as absolute being, the principle of consciousness, and peace. It remains without modification in all three states but is beclouded, like the sun, when thoughts, feelings and sensory perceptions occur. It is not then directly apprehended, but is indirectly experienced through the sense of personal existence, the consciousness of objects, whether these appear to be physical or mental, and appetence, whose ultimate aim is always the cessation of

---

3. Trances in which mind is active, where visions, for example, are seen, or voices heard, no matter of what nature, and whether or not they are prophetic, belong to the domain of duality and are therefore to be classed with other states of duality. The only exception to this rule is when something in the nature of what is described in Ch. XXIV, "The Verbal Expression of Non-Duality," occurs.

desire, that is to say, unconditioned peace. These matters will be examined in the third and fourth parts of this book. Meantime, we must consider the nature of objective experience, that is to say, of waking and dreaming experience.

PART TWO

OBJECTIVE EXPERIENCE

–IV–

Introduction to the Analysis of Objective Experience

Objective Experience

Objective experience is a blend of thinking and feeling. The nature of feeling cannot be understood until thought as such has been fully analyzed. By a thought as such, I mean the formal product of cognition, whether voluntary or involuntary.

The Two Kinds of Cognition

Cognition is either introversive or extroversive, that is to say, subjective or objective. Pure introversion takes us immediately beyond mentation. This is because a thought and its object, whatever that object may be, are inseparably one.[1] If, for example, we turn our attention towards absolute existence, which is the real self, objectivity vanishes and the thought merges in non-duality. And on the other hand, if our attention is turned towards sensory objects, the awareness of these objects constitutes so many objective thoughts. It is with this kind of thought that we are at present concerned.

---

1. We shall consider the nature of thoughts in greater detail in subsequent chapters.

A Thought Is Not an Entity

We shall see in a later chapter that thought is the name we give to the apparent objectification of consciousness. For the time being, however, we shall speak of thoughts as though they were real entities, since plain men regard them as such.

Abstract Thought and Generalization

Before proceeding to our examination of extroversion, let us pause awhile to see what is meant by abstract thought and generalization, and so prevent misunderstanding. They are linked to sensory perception, for in order to attain abstraction or generalization, we must consider particulars; and the actual thought that results is always in terms of the senses, no matter how abstract that thought may be or by what intuition it may have been arrived at. As an example, *man* is used in the title of this book to denote the characteristics of the human state. But no sooner is the word apprehended than some kind of visual representation appears, however vaguely, before the mind's eye.[2] Similarly, all abstract notions, whether they refer to qualities, numbers, relations, or concepts, require the support of some object of sensory perception, even if it be only a symbol such as a cipher or a sound. Abstract thoughts and generalizations are therefore the objects of consciousness. As such, they are quite distinct from introversion.

The Objects of Consciousness

An object of consciousness may be defined as whatever can recur in memory, for we remember only those things we have known.

---

2. With some people, the reaction may not be visual, but in any case it is sensory.

Sensory Perception

Objects as such are never actually perceived. Sensory perception gives us no more than the bare sensations of sound, touch,[3] light,[4] taste and smell: it does not present us with ready-made notions of objects. How from simple sensations we form the complex notion of an external world bound by time, space and causality will be the theme of the second part of our Inquiry.

---

3. I use the word *touch* to include all kinds of cutaneous sensations, *i.e.*, prick, pain, temperature, touch and kinesthesia. I would emphasize that this Inquiry has little to do with the aims of academic physiology and psychology, its purpose being wholly different from that of empirical science. The five categories of cutaneous sensation listed are borrowed from Parsons, *An Introduction to the Theory of Perception*, page 72 (Cambridge, 1927).

4. I use *light* as the most general term for form, shape and color, that is to say, for all that is visual.

–V–

Sensory Perception and the Notion of Objects

How the Notion of an Object Arises

I have just now stated that sensory perceptions give us no more than the bare sensations of sound, touch, light, taste and smell. If the percipient is repeatedly and similarly affected by a more or less constant group of sensations, he forms the notion of a specific object, or kind of objects.

The Correlation of Sense-Objects and the Senses

Light is inseparable from, and therefore one with, the act of seeing. Sound is inseparable from, and therefore one with, the act of hearing. The same stimulus may give rise to sensations of sound in the language of the ears, or of touch, light, taste and smell in the language of the skin, the eyes, the tongue or the nose. But this is not to say that what stimulates sensory perception has any real existence apart from its being perceived. If we abstract from our notion of an independently existing object the qualities our senses have given it, its materiality and objectivity vanish: and what remains is nameless, formless being.[1] In terms of the senses, something no doubt has been apprehended: but that something, in reality, is not an object: it transcends the duality of knower and known. Now

---

1. *Form* stands for sensible qualities in general, *name* for intellectual qualities, that is to say, for all that concerns the association of ideas and the notion of a specific object, or kind of objects.

the abstraction of sensible qualities from a foreign object implies that its perceiver has, in the process, transcended the sensible qualities of his person. And in the absence of sensible qualities both in the one and the other, it is not possible to find any difference between the perceiver and the perceived. We unwittingly make this abstraction whenever we cease to be conscious of objects, either in the interval between two thoughts, when a desire is fulfilled (as we shall see in Part Four), or in dreamless sleep.

These considerations prove that appearances as such are nothing more than the senses' sensing. The nameless, formless being to which I have referred is another aspect of the non-dual principle of consciousness. Why non-duality should seem to become divided into a conscious subject and its object is not at present our concern.

The Oneness of the Perceiver and the Perceived

I shall now restate the last section in other words. Between what is commonly called a sense-datum and its corresponding sense-organ, there is an immediate and inseparable connection. It is in the nature of the visual faculty to manifest shapes and colors, of the auditory faculty to manifest sounds; and so on. What we take to be an object is the visibility of vision, the audibility of hearing and the rest. But no object as such has been cognized.

Now although we habitually take the opposite view, the idea that sensations are caused by stimuli external to the senses is an illusion: this we have already seen in the previous section. Let the reader try to imagine the sort of world it would be if he had, instead of five, only four senses, and for example, if he had absolutely no sense of touch: it would certainly not be the same world whose real existence we now take for granted. Our notion of objects cannot therefore be separated from the acts of hearing, touching, seeing, tasting and smelling. Furthermore, our analysis of waking and dreaming has shown us that when these two states are looked at from the vantage-point of the consciousness which is common to both, they are indistinguishable: the experience of each one is a mental product. That being so, there is at no time a stimulus external to the senses.

The Relation between Brain, Sense-Organs and the Outer World

"A characteristic phenomenon in the relation between brain, sense-organs and the outer world is that of projection. Though sensations are appreciated as the result of changes in the brain-cells, they are felt as if taking place more remotely; touch is projected to the skin surface, taste to the mouth, while we regard sight and sound as coming from the surroundings. They are, as it were, conventional delusions established in infancy. For, in fact, our sensations are the mere masks and symbols of reality, which is filtered through our sensory recording apparatus."[2] Our author has previously stated that "the particular nature of a sensation is determined by the receiving organ, and not by the stimulus."[3] In the first of these notable passages, I find confirmation from the realm of empirical science that appearance as such is nothing more than the senses' sensing, though its author probably had no such intention; and in the second, that sense-objects are one with sensory perception.

At this stage, I must define reality, since the term has just now been introduced. Reality I define as that which

---

2. *Physiology,* by A. D. Le Vay, page 175 (English Universities Press, 1951).

3. Le Vay, *op. cit.,* page 175.

transcends change (see XXIII, note 1). Analysis of dreamless sleep, in the third chapter, showed this immutable reality to be the self, the self being that single consciousness in which the many and various aspects of objective experience come and go. Now it is true that "our sensations are the mere masks and symbols of reality." But having defined reality, I would add that we cannot have an *objective* knowledge of reality, which for us is identical with non-duality.

How the Notion of a World Arises

Objects as such are not perceived: they exist only as notions, that is to say, they exist when they are thought of and not otherwise. Now we cannot have more than a single thought at a time, although the rapidity with which thoughts succeed one another makes plain men believe the contrary.[4] It follows that the simultaneous existence of objects is an impossibility. But we remember our past notions and it is memory therefore that makes us believe in the coexistence of objects.[5] The illusion of the simultaneous and independent existence of objects gives rise to the notion of a world.[6] In this connection, I would refer the reader to my remarks about abstract thought and generalization (IV, Abstract Thought and Generalization): the notion of a world is a generalization and nothing more.

---

4. The idea that we can cognize several objects simultaneously is one of the many erroneous habits of thought that becloud our understanding. The exposure of such habits will be found to play an important part in the present Method.

5. The nature of memory will be discussed at a later stage.

6. By "independent," I refer to the idea that objects exist independently of their being cognized.

Conclusion: Sensations as the Words of a Sensory Language

When there is no objectification of consciousness, when in other words there is no sensory perception, what seemed to be an object loses both its sensory and intellectual attributes, remaining as the principle of consciousness in which it seemed to appear. It cannot then be called an object; nor, in reality, was there ever one, for in itself it transcended name and form. I do not mean to say that when a something is cognized, nothing whatsoever is present. When a something is cognized, a something does certainly exist, but not as it appears, for the appearance is determined solely by the percipient and not by the thing in itself. The senses are like so many languages, which express in their own idiom the unobjectified being that is beyond the domain of expression.

Postscript: A Word about Intuition

The following observations are not included in the main text of this chapter, since they anticipate a part of the Method which cannot be broached without further preparation. Readers who cannot for the present grasp their import are advised not to make undue efforts to do so, but rather to wait until they have read all the chapters up to and including the one on "Desires, Feelings, and the Witness" (XXIX). By that time all obstacles to understanding should have been removed. This is not a caprice on the author's part; and he may as well aver, that there are some passages in this book which will be fully comprehended only after the Method has been seen as a whole. To enjoy a melody, we must first hear it out. Then only can we look back at each detail and appreciate the mutual balance and the significance of all the notes, or groups of notes, that together constitute a melodic line.

In this and the previous chapter, mention has been made of intuition. Different people give different meanings to the word. By intuition I refer to the unwitting practice of introversion (IV, The Two Kinds of Cognition), which refers back all objective experience to subjective consciousness. It is a gift, and one which may often be developed by proper training. It cannot be held responsible for the rightness or the wrongness of the conclusions arrived at, nor does it bear any immediate relation to the degree of scholarly or aesthetic culture acquired by persons endowed in this manner. Culture may help to prevent, but it may also lead to, false conclusions. Something more than culture is therefore needed if intuitions are not to be misinterpreted by those who have them. This guidance will be discussed in Chapter XXIV.

The training I spoke of just now is the practice of introversion that forms an important part of the Vedantic method. It helps to lead to a state where intuition, instead of remaining fortuitous, becomes the normal pattern of experience. But this state transcends what is normally thought of as intuition: it may best be described as the realization of non-duality.[7]

---

7. Although there are probably many gifted persons who could if they wished follow this path, I need hardly say that the number of those who more than anything else desire spiritual knowledge is very small. "You can take a horse to water, but you can't make it drink!"

–VI–

The Body and the Sensory Faculty

The Body and Its World

The body could not exist without the senses; and the senses require the support of a body. The body and the sensory faculty are therefore inseparable. One may observe this upon waking, when awareness of foreign bodies is seen to be allied with awareness of one's own body. The percipient's body and world form an indivisible whole.

One's Body an Object of Consciousness

The plain man knows of subjectivity only through his experience of objects; and the objective side of experience is sensory (IV, Abstract Thought and Generalization). For him, therefore, the sensory faculty and its supporting body seem naturally to be on the side of subjective consciousness. This makes him think of his body as a thing apart; but body is merely an object of consciousness, one amongst others.

One's Body a Notion

Moreover, if it be true that objects as such are not perceived (V, How the Notion of an Object Arises), then one's own body as such, being an object, is not perceived. One's body is a notion, formed in the same manner as the notion of any other object.

– VII –

The Sensory Nature of the World

The Relation between the Percipient's Body and Foreign Bodies

The sensations that give rise to the notion of an object are nothing more than the senses' sensing. And because the senses cannot exist without the support of a body, it follows that our notion of any foreign body, whether animate or inanimate, depends upon the notion of our own body. When, for instance, we examine the notion of any particular object, its shape and color are found to be inseparably connected with our eyes, its feel, weight and temperature with our skin, its sound with our ears, and so on. Even to speak of *its* sound, color or feel is only a concession to a prejudice, for, in the actual experience, we are conscious simply of isolated sensations: it is afterwards that we call them the attributes of an object. Moreover, it is our body which provides the ultimate standard of size and situation.

The Notion of Other Persons' Bodies

We have seen that other people's bodies, like our own, are notions pertaining to the particular state of mental activity which is at present being experienced (III, The Objection Refuted). The same conclusion has been reached by an analysis of sensory perception, for the notion of a foreign body depends upon the notion of our own body, whether it be the body of waking or of dreaming experience. We shall now find that the experience we attribute to others is also a notion, in so far as its objectivity is concerned.

– VIII –

Common Sense and the Testimony of Others

The Limitations of Common Sense

Common sense relies upon the testimony of other living beings, or of man-made adjuncts to the sensory faculty, in order to prove the independent existence of objects. It takes for granted, moreover, the independent existence of the living beings, or the mechanical devices, upon whose testimony it relies. Against the commonsense view, in total opposition, stands the metaphysical, according to which the idea that objects exist independently of their being perceived, whether they be animate or inanimate, is illusory.

Now we need not, and indeed we cannot, disregard the canons of common sense in the purely human situations to which they apply. But if, as this Method postulates, we would become centered in the immutable self instead of living on a periphery and falling a prey to whatever affects our person, we must adopt a position that will enable us to view with complete objectivity all the aspects of our experience: in this way alone can we discriminate between its transient and its imperishable sides. Such a view is not to be had excepting from the vantage-point of consciousness.

The Attribution of Life to Other Bodies

I have just now made a passing reference to animate and inanimate bodies, between which no certain distinction can always be made. The senses as such meet solely with insentient matter; and the principle of life and consciousness can never be the object of perception.[1]

Other embodied beings seem to exist only when we ourselves seem to be embodied. Embodiment is experienced in the states of waking and dreaming. These states are not permanent: they come and go in consciousness. The experience of the one corresponds exactly to the experience of the other, both being the products of mind. If the imaginary bodies we encounter in dreams are endowed with life and consciousness by the dreaming subject, so also, by the waking subject, are those we encounter in the waking-state. Thus the habit of attributing life to bodies goes hand in hand with extroversion; and the notion of a living organism is nothing but an objectification of the principle of life in terms of the senses.

Conclusion: A Means to Rising above the Commonsense Outlook

Just as we cannot gauge the exact color of objects if we always wear tinted spectacles, we cannot know the true nature of our individual experience if we persist in viewing it from the standpoint of individuality. Thus the commonsense outlook must be surpassed if we would understand our individual experience aright. Common sense, in truth, is synonymous

---

1. Bertrand Russell, adopting the standpoint of common sense, has defined a living organism as that which possesses the capacity to form conditioned reflexes. This may provide an excellent criterion for the inferences of natural science: it explains nothing about the attribution of life to foreign bodies.

with ignorance: and ignorance breeds doubt. As a practical measure, therefore, we would do well to seek the motive of every philosophical question. If its purpose was to elicit an answer tending to establish the validity of the commonsense, waking, point of view, we should reconsider the whole problem from the standpoint of consciousness, when it can be seen in its proper perspective, or else it may vanish. Something in us is sure to set up a clamor of "yes, but . . . ," "all the same . . . ," and the rest of its artillery, but that will not deter us: our motive is the quest for truth.[2]

---

2. This "something" is the ego. Its nature will be discussed at the proper time.

The Unreal Dualism of Mind
and Matter

No Distinction between the Mental and the Physical

At the beginning of this work, we anticipated that waking experience, like the experience of dreaming, is a product of the mind (II, A Further Comparison of Waking and Dreaming). This has now been proved, for we have found that all sense-objects, including our body, exist solely as notions, in other words, that they exist only when thought of. Thus the distinction between physical and mental objects is unreal: the difference lies, not in the nature of the objects, but in the different quality, or intensity, of thoughts. Extroversion seems at one time to assume tangibility and at another it does not.

Insoluble Problems

I am not prepared to essay an answer to the question why this should be so, for it would necessitate an excursion into the fields of cosmogony and evolution; and that would be to concede that appearances as such existed independently of their being cognized, an error I have disproved. Nothing, moreover, could possibly be gained from such a concession: if we were to fall back upon some outside principle by way of explaining the origin of manifestation, we would still be unable to find any reason why that first cause, God, which may be supposed to want nothing, should have wished a universe into being. Rather than toy with these insoluble problems to no purpose, I shall demonstrate, in due course, that all questions regarding origins are illogical and absurd.[1]

1. I have discussed cosmogony and evolution, from various standpoints, in my *Immediate Knowledge and Happiness* (John Watkins, London, 1951), and notably in the chapter on "Evolution." We shall consider the question of origins in Ch. XXVIII.

$-X-$

Two Common Misunderstandings

Bishop Berkeley, Bertrand Russell, and Dr. Samuel Johnson

Bertrand Russell, writing about the philosophy of Berkeley,[1] remarks that "although Berkeley is right in saying that the events we know immediately are mental, it is highly probable that he is wrong as to the events we infer in places where there are no living bodies." Lord Russell allows such a probability because "light and sound take time to travel from their sources to the percipient, and one must suppose that something is happening along the route by which they travel. What is happening along the route is presumably not 'mental,' for, as we have seen, 'mental' events are those that have peculiar mnemic effects which are connected with living tissue." I am unable to see any difference between "the events we know immediately" and those "we infer in places where there are no living bodies," for in postulating events we do not or cannot actually perceive, we inevitably visualize mental images which therefore "we know immediately," even if vaguely, as though they were physically before us, granting the dualism of mind

---

1. An *Outline of Philosophy*, pages 257-8.

and matter which Russell has elsewhere disproved.[2] And in this postulation, imaginatively with our own body, vicariously through another's or through some recording apparatus, we are present to witness the inferred events, no matter whether the inference be right or wrong.

In the same book, Lord Russell states that "matter has very definitely come down in the world as a result of recent physics. It used to be the cause of our sensations: Dr. Johnson 'disproved' Berkeley's denial by kicking a stone. If he had known that his foot never touched the stone, and that both were complicated systems of wave-motions, he might have been less satisfied with this refutation. We cannot say that 'matter' is the cause of our sensations."[3] This, I must point out, is merely to substitute one terminology for another. The proper reply is that Johnson's foot formed an integral part of the seemingly external world and as such was not different from the stone. And if the stone was mental, so was the body. He made the mistake I have already mentioned in thinking of his body as a thing apart (VI, One's Body an Object of Consciousness).

---

2. Bertrand Russell, *The Analysis of Matter*: "As regards the world in general, both physical and mental, everything that we know of its intrinsic character is derived from the mental side, and almost everything that we know of its causal laws is derived from the physical side. But from the standpoint of philosophy, the distinction between physical and mental is superficial and unreal."

3. *Ibid.*, page 290.

– XI –

The Illusion of Materiality

Materiality

Our notion of materiality coincides with the twin illusions that objects exist independently of their being perceived; and that these objects, whether solid, liquid or gaseous, consist of three dimensions. In order to understand how the notion of a three-dimensional object arises, it will be necessary first to understand how we form the notion of extension in length and breadth.

Length and Breadth

Extension, in length, in breadth, or in both together, is an idea formed by our memory of discontinuous though successive sensations which, from the commonsense standpoint, may appear either as physical or mental. These sensations give us the impression that we have perceived a surface. But there has been no immediate perception of a surface.

As an example, let the reader behold this printed page, held at reading distance.[1] He will notice that the eyes or the page must be moved if more than a very limited portion is to be seen: and that while he observes one portion, he cannot

---

1. I say "at reading distance," because it often happens that what afterwards is called a surface falls within the field of a single visual or tactile focus of attention. In such cases, we either look or feel more minutely, or else, and this is the most usual, we unwittingly call on past experience to supply imaginatively the sensations that combine to form the notion of a surface or an object.

observe the others. Thus the impression of having seen a page is not the product of a single, comprehensive glance. It derives from the memory of several distinct glances. At this stage, we may usefully recall that if the percipient is repeatedly and similarly affected by a more or less constant group of sensations, he forms the notion of a specific object (V, How the Notion of an Object Arises).

Depth

Having found extension in length and breadth to be a notion, let us now consider extension in depth, or from a surface inwards. Our knowledge of this dimension likewise cannot be the result of direct perception, for sensations are of surfaces. Nevertheless, the idea of depth is inherent in the notion we have of surfaces, a surface without substance being quite inconceivable (IV, Abstract Thought and Generalization), whatever abstraction-mongers may tell us.

The Physiological Aspect of Tridimensionality

The notion of depth has its physiological basis in two parallel factors, the conventions of the sense of touch and binocular vision, the second being impossible without the first. Binocular vision "provides the stereoscopic effect, the appreciation of depth and distance; this depends on the fact that the images of an object formed by each eye are slightly different and that these two images are presented simultaneously to the brain without appearing double."[2] So that we may understand in what way two distinct images, that is to say, two distinct perceptions, come to appear in consciousness as one, let us examine a similar process performed in the brain with respect to

---

2. Le Vay, *op. cit.*, pages 179-80.

tactile sensations, since it can easily be verified. "The skin offers a good instance of how our conventional reading of sensations ('the words of a sensory language,' V, Conclusion: Sensations as the Words of a Sensory Language) depends merely upon habituation. A pencil slid between the tips of the middle and index finger is felt as one stimulus because these surfaces are normally adjacent and we have learnt to fuse their sensations; but, if the fingers are crossed, surfaces which are never normally in contact are brought together and a pencil placed between them is now felt as double."[3] In this case, association does not occur automatically, as is normal; instead of the two sensations appearing as one, two separate sensations are experienced. If we did not have the testimony of our eyes or the knowledge of the experiment we were making, the two sensations would remain, as in fact they are, quite discrete. This should now be applied to the faculty of grasping, in which the physiological basis of tridimensionality certainly lies. But it must be clear from these considerations that the physiological aspect of perception cannot be separated from the psychological. This will be dealt with in due course.

Continuity

The response to sensory stimuli that exceed a certain minimum threshold continues for a brief period after the event. Ultimately this response is cerebral and belongs to the domain of biochemistry. In normal circumstances, distinct groups of sensations, and their prolongation, succeed one another with sufficient rapidity to make them appear as though they formed an unbroken line. There will, however, be no difficulty in understanding that objective continuity is an illusion, if what was said regarding the interval between two

---

3. Le Vay, *op. cit.*, page 185.

thoughts be borne in mind (III, The Interval between Two Thoughts). We do not normally take note of this interval because we wrongly assume that when nothing objective is present to consciousness, what subsists is nothingness and not consciousness. The sense of continuity cannot therefore be derived from the objective, physiological side of perception; it is derived from the single, immutable and non-temporal consciousness in which all perceptions occur, as we shall see in a later chapter.

The Psychological Origin of Tridimensionality

When our attention goes outward, we become conscious of sensations and instinctively perform the mental process described in the second article of this chapter, completing it with another, which is to imagine what we cannot possibly perceive, namely, the other side or the inside of the surface we perceive notionally.[4] We then gain the impression of having perceived a three-dimensional object. Our habit of combining tactile with visual and other sensations is due partly, if not wholly, to the fact that we are able to have the feeling of, or touch, those parts of our body we cannot see: analogy does the rest. As an illustration of how we create the appearance of the world, we need only look at a painting and ask ourselves

---

4. In practice, we do not always actually see or feel in imagination the other side or the inside of a surface, the idea of materiality being so much a part of our mental habit that we do not need to. In sensory perception, as in ratiocination, even those who are least developed among us often arrive at conclusions by an elliptical process which is probably the best measure of good and bad brains. While this Method is being practiced, it may be necessary to disentangle ourselves at first from this pragmatically useful but metaphysically unreliable short cut.

where the recognition of nonexistent objects in a non-existent space comes from. It does not come from the colored canvas: it comes from our habit of associating physically experienced and imaginary sensations to form ideas. The solid world of the five senses is created by us in the same way.[5]

The Aim of This Analysis

I have given a very simplified account of a complex process, for this work, as already stated (IV, note 3), is written from a point of view and with a purpose differing essentially from the standpoint of empirical science. My aim here is to separate from the objective side of human experience the conscious principle that informs it. The meaning of sensory perception and of memory will be discussed at a later stage when we come to analyze the nature of desire.

Summary

From all these considerations, it is evident that materiality is an illusion created by the combination through memory of visual and tactile sensations, whether these are experienced as physical or mental, relative to actual and imaginary movements of the perceiver's body and senses.

---

5. As a further illustration, and towards completing what was said about the attribution of life and consciousness to others (Ch. VIII), let me cite the sound-film. Out of the mechanical play of light on a screen and the vacuous sound-waves that fill the hall during its projection, we create for ourselves, as in a dream, a living world in which we participate entirely, running up and down the whole vast gamut of thought and feeling.

– XII –

Space

The Concept of Space and the Illusion of Materiality

The notion of a world, as we have seen (V, How the Notion of a World Arises), has its origin in the illusion that objects, themselves merely present notions, have an independent and simultaneous existence. This illusion, together with that of tridimensionality, gives rise to the notion of a space in which material things are located and by which they are pervaded. In the interval separating these supposedly coexistent bodies, there is nothing that corresponds to the common notion of an object. This vacant interval, moreover, by comparison with the combined volume of all visible, tangible bodies, seems to be immeasurably great and wholly independent. To this visually vacant space, plain men ascribe absolute existence. But we cannot think of an interval or a vacancy in the abstract, that is to say, we cannot think of space without reference to tangible bodies, beginning always with our own. It follows that space, far from its having an independent and absolute existence, coincides with the notion of matter; and in particular, it coincides with the notion of our own incarnation.

Distance and Proximity

In other words, the concept of space and the erroneous idea that objects have an independent and simultaneous existence go hand in hand. When this has not been understood, the following question is often asked, usually with a look and a tone of supreme triumph: "If objects are notions that arise and abide solely in my head, should not a distant object, when I think of it, appear just before me here?" The question is based on a misunderstanding. Determinative thoughts as to time and place do not always accompany the thought of an object, though they almost invariably do, and that with such rapidity as to make the question seem plausible at first sight (XI, Continuity). Yet the object itself, when we are specifically thinking about it, has no location, that is to say, we do not think of it as being near or far, here or there: the notion of the object is alone present to consciousness. It needs a separate thought, or series of thoughts, to situate the object in relation to others: this will be evident if we consider the sort of sensory impressions spontaneously evoked by the words "here" and "there." And besides, the same memory which makes us believe in the simultaneous existence of objects will not allow us to see Vesuvius on a writing desk!

At this stage, I would again remind my readers of what has been said about abstract thinking (IV, Abstract Thought and Generalization). Space, location, distance, proximity and direction are so many abstract terms arising out of present perceptions, without which they would be meaningless. These convenient generalities we tend to convert into absolute entities.[1] It must never be forgotten that whenever we use such words, we are speaking of actual images or sensations, however vague they may be, for there is no difference between mental and physical awareness.

---

1. It is not unlikely that the use, in this treatise, of expressions such as consciousness, the principle of consciousness, peace, and non-duality, will be taken as examples of the tendency I have referred to. I am confident that readers who harbor any such idea will be disabused of it if only they have the patience to read on right up to the end of this book.

Conclusion

From these considerations, an important fact emerges. If material objects and their spatial situation are seen as separate notions linked only by memory, that is to say, in the mind, it must be clear that objects are situated, not in some invisible and external space, but in the consciousness of their perceiver.[2]

---

2. That the absolute existence of a three-dimensional space is no longer accepted by physics without many reservations is of real importance, since it confirms the findings of Adwaita Vedanta. The same may be said regarding the rejection of the commonsense notion of time and the emergence of a theory of time-space conceived as a four-dimensional continuum. But when the classical concept of tridimensionality has been discarded, why is it thought necessary to postulate a four-dimensional continuum, which perpetuates, in a new form, the old commonsense illusions of the real and independent existence of things? I would not for a moment deny the practical advantage that such a concept is said to bring to empirical science: I can only say that it has little meaning for psychology and none at all so far as this doctrine is concerned. I maintain that this continuum, if it may still be so called, is the single consciousness in which all our manifold experience occurs, as the concluding words of this chapter show.

–XIII–

The Illusions of Causality

Change

A characteristic of waking and dreaming experience is that of mutation. But nothing, in truth, changes, for when the prototype has changed, it has ceased to exist. In other words, if the object supposedly altered has ceased to exist in its previous form, we cannot then say that the present form is anything but a new form, that is, another and original object of consciousness: A question may arise whether records taken of the original, or our memories of it, do not provide an adequate basis for comparing and associating the two objects, the old and the new. But a photograph, for example, can only be an extension to memory, when it is not simply a substitute. And as for the ideas of plain men regarding the nature of memory, they are based on a misunderstanding, as we shall see in due course. Remembrance is merely one kind of thought amongst others, each memory forming the present, and therefore an entirely new, object of consciousness.

Cause and Effect

It is impossible to live in the world unless we accept causality, but it is impossible to understand the nature of the world when causality is accepted. Its acceptance amounts to granting the independent and simultaneous existence of objects, any one of which may be acted upon by another. This we have seen to be an impossibility, for an object cannot exist unless it is thought of (IX, No Distinction between the Mental and the Physical), and two thoughts cannot occur simultaneously. If, however, we grant for argument's sake that objects could exist independently of their being cognized, we should still be unable to allow the relation of cause and effect. Strictly speaking, it is only after the occurrence that we can take it to be the effect of a cause, by which time the ostensible cause must be presumed to have passed over entirely into the effect, the two never having been observed in concert. Causality is therefore a meaningless term.

Relationship

Notwithstanding the fact that all men experience the self as an unbroken continuity, they normally take no note of its existence excepting as the subject to whom objects appear discontinuously. This is to be expected, for they have not looked into the nature of dreamless sleep. Moreover, because they always emphasize the objective side of their experience and overlook the subjective, they transfer the continuity of consciousness to the objects of consciousness in the form of relationship. Consciousness then appears as the memory which relates one thought to another. But remembrance, as already stated, is only one kind of thought: and two thoughts cannot occur simultaneously.

Summary: The Illusion of Relationship

A thought is the consciousness of an object and every new thought bespeaks a new object. Since two thoughts cannot together occur, it follows that two objects cannot coexist. How then could they be related? Thus the ideas of change and causality are erroneous, for the incident of change, or the relation of a cause to its effect, is a figment.

–XIV–

Time and Space

The Relation of Space to Time

Granting the reality of space when the reality of the percipient's body is also granted, several perceptions are required in order that the notion of an extension may be formed (XI, Length and Breadth).

These several perceptions take time; that is to say, they are successive. Space is therefore inseparably linked to time, and time to the memory of successive perceptions, granting also the real existence of a retentive faculty.

The Concept of Time

". . . Many thinkers . . . believe that the concept of time cannot be fully accounted for, unless we distinguish between perceptual, or subjective, time, which is confined to the perpetually shifting 'now' of the present, and conceptual, or objective, time, which includes all periods of time and in which events we call past, present and future can be mutually and fixedly related."[1] But no clear distinction can be drawn between perceptual and conceptual time, for the one cannot be postulated without the other. Nevertheless, if we consider the "now" of the present entirely by itself, just as it occurs in experience, time need not be postulated at all. And if we closely examine our ideas of past, present and future, they are

---

1. R. B. Winn, in the *Dictionary of Philosophy* (Philosophical Library, New York, 1942).

found to be gratuitous, and so again we cannot postulate time. Both points will be explained in what follows.

–XV–

Time and Timelessness

Duration and the Notion of Time

As I have already observed (III, Sleeping Experience, a), dreamless sleep is a state of unconditioned being, when viewed from its own standpoint and in reality. We say, nevertheless, that we slept for so many hours, just as we describe as brief the interval between two thoughts. In both cases, we attribute an existence in time to the unconditioned self. But if we carefully consider the actual experience, we shall find that duration has no part in it: we experience duration only in states characterized by the succession of thoughts. Time is therefore the object of consciousness: time, in other words, has no existence unless we are thinking of it; and our concept of time is based on the ideas of past, present and future.

Now this division of time, as I shall demonstrate in the next chapter, has no real meaning. The thought of a past or a future event occurs always as the present object of consciousness; and the event we supposedly recall or expect must have been, or will be, a present experience. Strictly speaking, moreover, a past event as such has vanished once and for all; a future event as such is wholly inexistent. It follows that in thinking of past and future occurrences, we do so only with reference to a present time. But without a subsistent past and future we could not form any notion of the present. There cannot indeed be a present, since there is neither a past nor a future time. Consciousness alone subsists and consciousness alone is ever-present.

Time

From a standpoint that is still in duality, thought appears as the principle of consciousness objectified, objectified by what I do not say, for in order that consciousness may seem to be objectified, an independent agent is needed: and nothing can exist independently of consciousness.[1] Let me then repeat, in the only terms available, that thought is the apparent objectification of consciousness. Let me add, moreover, that each thought as such has an object and that the two are inseparable. Now time, or the notion of succession, is one such object: and time too is consciousness objectified.

The Passage of Time and Pure Being

We measure the passage of time by the observation of movements in natural objects like the sun. Observation implies the remembrance of successive sensory perceptions. Were it not for these memories, our notion of time, if we could ever have acquired it, would fade into the experience of pure being, as it does whenever mental activity ceases.

The Apprehension of Timelessness

The absence of mental activity cannot properly be called a state, since it transcends time. If we wish to understand what it is, we must abstract every idea of duration from our mind. This is not impossible, for a thought as such is always at one with its object. If we make timelessness the object of thought,

---

1. Why the principle of consciousness, which is immutable and impersonal, should happen to become manifest as the duality of a conscious subject and its object is a question that will be considered in the chapter on "Absurd Questions."

all that is objective drops away and we realize timelessness as pure, changeless, being.

– XVI –

Time and the Present Eternity

The Situating of Experience in Time

As already stated, when we are thinking of a specific object, nothing else is present to consciousness and there is no idea then of the object's location. A separate thought, or series of thoughts, is required in order to situate that one object in relation to others. These determinative thoughts follow almost invariably (XII, Distance and Proximity). Likewise, just as one group of sensations going to form the notion of an object is followed habitually by another, which situates the object in space, so is this, and any other kind of experience, followed habitually by one which situates it in time, that is to say, it brings the experience into relation with the succession of thoughts in general. The group of thoughts so situated is then considered to be a present occurrence, though it is already past: it is considered to be a past occurrence only when new thoughts arise.[1]

---

1. See XIX, The Different Aspects of Thought, in connection with the use of "thought."

Past, Present and Future

I *thought* really means I *am at present conscious of the kind of thought called a memory* (or *a recollection*); I *shall think* really means I *am at present conscious of the kind of thought called an expectation* (or *an intention or a prediction*); I *think* really means I *am at present conscious of the kind of thought called an actuality or a present occurrence.* That the absence of objective experience cannot be thought or spoken of as a present occurrence is obvious: in the first place, there is no occurrence; and in the second, there is no individual to speak or to think, the seeming duality of a conscious subject and its object arising only when objective experience arises.

Sleep and Non-Duality

I *slept* (or I *was unconscious*) really means I *am at present conscious of a memory that relates to the absence of thought.* But it is not the absence as such of thought that is remembered. Sleep and unconsciousness are notions based on the memory of conditions that preceded and followed the cessation of individual experience. I say this from the standpoint of the plain man who thinks of sleep as occurring in time, that is to say, as having a beginning and an end, thus making it a part of waking experience; whereas sleep from its own standpoint cannot be said to occur at all. Profound sleep in itself is non-temporal and neither an active nor a passive state: duration, activity and passivity pertain exclusively to the objective realm which in deep sleep is non-existent. But some positive state, corresponding to what is negatively called the absence of thought, does undoubtedly exist. And though I call it a state, it is not a state in the common acceptation of the word, for states begin and end, but this is non-temporal. In it we are merged in non-duality, ready as it were to become, or rather to seem to become, the conscious subject, when objects are experienced, or seem to be experienced. Nevertheless, non-duality abides as the substratum and the reality of dualistic experience (III, The Singleness of Non-Mental Experience), though we cannot as individuals be aware of its existence when our attention is turned outwards.[2]

Time and the Present Eternity

Like space, which would be inconceivable apart from the objects it is supposed to pervade (XII, The Concept of Space and the Illusion of Materiality), time also cannot be more than a notion. It is never directly experienced. I mean by this that we never experience a present time: the present time is nothing more than our way of qualifying a select group of thoughts which has just now been present to consciousness. Behind our notion of a present time, however, is the immediate apprehension of the principle of consciousness, which is ever present as the self, not in terms of succession, but as the present eternity. And this immediate knowledge finds expression in our use of the pronoun, I, that is to say, in egoism.

Conclusion: The Ego and Non-Duality

In the final analysis, therefore, the pronoun, I, even when supposedly standing for individual consciousness, stands always for non-duality. If we would actualize this truth, we

---

2. I speak of the "existence of non-duality" figuratively. It is not a presence we can know as we know objects, since it is the real self, that is to say, the ultimate subject. I once heard a great Indian sage remark that non-duality, though unknowable, is of all things the best known, for it is ever experienced as the self.

must abstract from our notion of consciousness all that is personal, not as we unwittingly do when we fall asleep and between two thoughts, but by the remembrance in our workaday life of the main principles of Adwaita, so far only partially stated.[3]

---

3. I would strongly emphasize that no one should attempt to apply these principles by himself: the method is different in each individual case. Personal guidance from one who has fully realized non-duality is therefore essential. Neither this nor any other book can take its place. My aim here is to indicate a practical possibility which a few happy members of the human species must always have known and experienced.

PART THREE

THE SELF

The Definition of a Human Being

Individuality and Personality

A practical definition of individuality is the consciousness of a separate, corporeal existence; and of personality, the sum of physical and mental traits characterizing that individual existence.

The Self

Now in the being conscious of something, there is a distinction between consciousness and the object of consciousness. We are conscious of our individual existence and therefore we transcend it. That which transcends individual existence is the changeless, impersonal self. Notwithstanding, we identify the self with the body.

Personal Identity

The outcome of this mistaken attachment is the notion of a personal identity, to which we give indirect expression through the possessive and direct expression through the personal and reflexive pronouns. Body continually changes, but we who claim it as our own are changeless, otherwise we could not say, *This portrait is of me as a child.* Yet we ignore the evidence and become identified with each successive bodily state of which we are conscious. This ignorance causes us to personify the immutable self as *our* self, that is to say, as I who think, know, enjoy, perceive by the senses, and act, and their opposites.

The Immutable Self

A doubt may arise whether the self may properly be called changeless, even though it does not change as the body changes. But change is a characteristic of matter. The self, since it transcends the body, transcends change, including birth and death.

The Definition of a Human Being

Our notion of individual existence is born of the identification of self and body. This identification is mistaken, because the changeless self and a changeful body cannot be identical. Typical expressions of identification are, *I am of medium height, This portrait is of me as a child, I am hungry, I injured my leg, My body is lean,* and *I lost myself.* This supposed identity of incompatibles is called a human being.

–XVIII–

Identification

The Personal Pronoun and Identification

Plain men use the pronoun, *I*, indifferently to express three distinct levels of identification. First, identification with the body and the bodily senses, for example, *I am of medium height* and *I hear*. Second, with thoughts and the affections, for example, *I think* or *I imagine*, and *I am happy* or *I am moved*. Third, with the state of unconsciousness supposed to exist in the absence of thought, for example, *I was unconscious* or *I slept soundly*.

The Personal Pronoun and Unconsciousness

The expression, *I was unconscious*, is a contradiction in terms. It means *I, the thinker, had no thoughts*. But I cannot be a thinker when I have no thoughts. When thought is absent, I remain in being although the consciousness of an individual existence has vanished with the cessation of mental activity. Thus the expressions, *I was unconscious, or shall be unconscious,* imply that *I continued, or shall continue, to exist without individuality*. Every human life proves this fact, although it is not recognized. If, for example, there were any fear lest the loss of individual consciousness spelt annihilation, no one who identified himself with his body would dare to fall asleep.[1]

---

1. The same may be said of general anesthesia, once it has been experienced.

The Personal Pronoun and Consciousness

As human beings, we seem to have a personal identity that is expressed by the pronoun, *I*. This ego causes the real self to appear as identical with the body, the senses, or the mind. Such an identification is wholly illogical and unreal. The personal pronoun, whatever sense we may give it, denotes always the immutable self, that single consciousness in which the totality of objective experience seems to occur. *I think* means *I am conscious of thoughts; I see or hear* means *I am conscious of visual or auditory perceptions;* and *I am happy* means *I am conscious of a feeling of happiness.*

Consciousness and Mental Activity

The Different Aspects of Thought

I use the terms *thinker, thinking* and *thought* in what follows to include all the different aspects of mental activity as such, that is to say, reasoning and intellection, imagination, feeling, volition, and perception, the latter denoting the "mental action of knowing external things through the medium of sense presentations."[1] To this list must be added one other, namely, egoism or the habit of identification. I call it the I-thought. This, together with its concomitant, memory, will be studied in due course.

Mental Activity Defined

Mental activity is a notion arising from the memory of distinct thoughts. And since each thought as such constitutes an object of consciousness, I shall in future speak, whenever possible, of *objective* or *individual experience* in preference to *mental activity.*

Thought

Thoughts are so called from the standpoint of one who sporadically identifies himself with his body, since his own and other bodies appear as external to what he takes to be himself, while thoughts seem to occur within. But for one who

---

1. Cassell's *New English Dictionary.*

has understood that the body and its world are merely notions pertaining to his individual experience, there is neither an inner nor an outer world: the whole objective domain will appear to be mental.

If it has been clearly understood that the commonsense distinction between matter and mind, or waking and dreaming, is an illusion, then the truth of this statement will be readily grasped. But if all its implications have not been fully accepted, we are likely to oscillate continually between identification with the body as such (*I am of medium height*) and identification with thoughts as such (*I am clever*). We shall continue to view thoughts as subtle entities until we shall have known by reasoning and accepted the implications of the fact that all the objects of consciousness, whether they appear as external or internal, are so many aspects of a single objective plane. And then we shall find it pointless to make any distinction between mental and sensory, or physical, activity. What is called a thought is the consciousness of something: and this consciousness we personify as *I who think*. But for all that, I shall continue to use the word *thought* for the sake of simplicity, so long as we are examining human experience as such.

The Thinker

The thinker is supposed to think the thoughts of which he is conscious. But no one thinks.

This truth will become apparent as we proceed; and in particular from our examination of the duality of subject and object, in the chapter to follow. It is enough for the time being to note that the expressions, *I think* and *I am thinking*, both mean *I am conscious of something objective* and not *I am the thinker*.

Conclusion

Whereas the objects of consciousness are many and various, the single consciousness in which they appear remains unmodified. I am therefore a principle transcending all that is objective to me. I cannot be the thinker, for the thinker as such is the object of consciousness and not the self, otherwise I could not remember having thought (IV, The Objects of Consciousness).

–XX–

The Illusion of Duality

Duality Defined

As already stated (III, Sleeping Experience, b), duality is the seeming division of non-dual consciousness into thinker and thought, or subject and object, the one being conscious of the other. We shall now see why duality is only a figment.

Subject and Object

When I am conscious of an object, that is, of a notion or a percept, that object alone is present. When I am conscious of my perceiving, what alone presents itself to consciousness is the notion that I perceive the object: and therefore the notion of my being the perceiver also constitutes an object of consciousness. From this, a most important fact emerges: the so-called subject who thinks, and its apparent object, have no immediate relation.

That the notions of subject and object are separate thoughts may be seen from the following example, drawn from everyday life. When we are absorbed in some activity, let us say in reading a book, we experience a steady flow of thoughts relating to its contents. The notion, *I am reading,* does not occur while we are thus absorbed: it occurs only when our attention wavers. I have given this example because its lesson is readily understood: a little reflection will show that even when we are not thus absorbed for any appreciable lapse of time, the subject who afterwards lays claim to the action was not present to consciousness when the action was taking place. The idea of our being the agent occurs to us as a separate thought, which is to say that it forms an entirely fresh object of consciousness. And since, at the time of the occurrence, we were present as neither the thinker, the agent, the percipient, nor the enjoyer, no subsequent claim on our part could alter the position. The cause of our claiming that which belongs to the body is to be found in the erroneous habit of identification.

Memory and Ignorance

If the notions of subject and object are both the separate objects of consciousness, neither term has any real significance. An object, in the absence of a subject, cannot be what is normally called an object; and the subject, in the absence of an object, cannot be what is normally called the subject. It is in memory that the two notions seem to combine to form an entirely new notion, *I am the perceiver or the thinker.*

Now all notions are more or less complex. Memory is therefore an ingredient essential to the sense of individuality. Individuality is the apparent combination of the changeless self and a changeful body. Ignorance I have elsewhere described as the identification of body and self and, as a corollary, the personification of the impersonal principle of consciousness (XVII, Personal Identity & The Definition of a Human Being).

–XXI–

Life, Memory and Desire

We remember that alone which has affected us: and what affects us is pleasure and pain. The memory of pleasure and pain gives rise to desire and aversion: these two in action become will. And will, or conation, in its widest sense, makes us seek what memory tells us has been found agreeable or necessary to life and avoid what has been found disagreeable or hurtful to it.[1]

Now life, or individual existence, is the expression of non-duality (III, Sleeping Experience, a & b): it proceeds in terms of desire and aversion. These, then, are also the expressions of non-duality, for the ultimate object of every desire is to become desireless (XXIX, Peace the Ultimate Object of Every Desire: see also III, Sleeping Experience, c). Aversion is simply the obverse of desire and has the same target. This manner of looking at pleasure and pain will be developed in a later chapter. Meanwhile, it is evident that the search for the one and the avoidance of the other are the sole and complementary aims of individual existence at all levels. Neither would be possible without memory.[2]

---

1. There will be no difficulty in applying what I have said regarding desire and aversion to the different modes of individual experience: we have seen that the commonsense distinction between mind and matter is unreal. I refer to the fact that we have desires which appear at times to be physical and at others mental.

2. It is the same thing whether these memories are conscious, unconscious or subconscious, whichever of the two last expressions is preferred. See Ch. II, n. 1.

– XXII –

The Origin of Memory, and the Witness

The Thinker an Object of Consciousness

I can remember only what I have known.[1] I remember not only my thoughts:[2] I remember also my having thought. It follows that I, as the thinker or individual, am the object of consciousness; but as the knower of this and of all other objects, it follows that I am consciousness itself.

Egoism and the Act of Remembering

Whenever the principle of consciousness gets identified with the body, the false notion of my being the thinker springs up. That which claims to have been conscious of an event at which it was not present is the ego, or the I-thought. Thus the ego can claim only what has gone before and the experience so claimed is a remembrance.

Memory and Identification

As just now stated, the false notion of my being the thinker arises whenever there is identification of the impersonal principle of consciousness and the body. The effect of this identification is to divide non-dual consciousness into the ostensible duality of a conscious subject and its object.

---

1. Whether the knowledge or the memory is correct or incorrect makes no difference.

2. See Ch. XIX, The Different Aspects of Thought.

Since the objects of consciousness appear discontinu-ously; and since, moreover, the conscious subject, made objec-tive in the form of the claiming I-thought, also appears discontinuously, the consciousness that illuminates them seems to be discontinuous too. When non-dual consciousness seems in this way to be conditioned by time, it seems to assume the form of a faculty of remembering that gives cohe-sion to what would otherwise be a state of total flux, unimag-inable and impossible because it could not be known by a knower who, by his having no continuity, must perforce change at every perception: he could not even know himself. Memory and the consciousness of individual existence are therefore synonymous.

Memory and the Witness

The consciousness of individual existence and memory are indeed synonymous.

But we look forward as well as back. Now although it is true that in looking forward we make use of past experience, it would nevertheless be more precise and comprehensive if we spoke of a witness that observes the stream of objective experi-ence as a whole rather than of a faculty which only remembers, since retention merely reflects the witness. This witness is what I have hitherto called the consciousness in which objects appear. It must not, as such, be identified with the principle of consciousness.

The Twofold Nature of the Ego, and the Witness

The apparent existence of a conscious, witnessing fac-ulty is made possible by the ego's double nature. The ego, or I-thought, which is engendered by an illusory combination of the self and the body, partakes of both, claiming sometimes to be the one and sometimes the other. When it claims that which belongs to the body, it causes the self to appear as active (*I am the doer, the thinker or the enjoyer*). When it claims that which belongs to the self, it causes the latter to appear as inactive (*I slept soundly and knew nothing, or I was unconscious*). But the self transcends both action and inaction, since it transcends the individual (XVII, The Self). And that is why, whenever individuality appears, the self assumes the role of an impassible witness.

–XXIII–

The Dissolution of Egoism and the Restitution of the Self

The Ego and the Non-Dual Self

The ego is not an entity: it is the highly complex notion of an embodied existence, arising out of the illusory combination of self and body. As stated above, it partakes of both, claiming sometimes to be the one and sometimes the other. I call the combination of self and body illusory, since the body, being changeful, is unreal.[1] If the changeful, bodily aspect of the ego is disclaimed, the ego as such dissolves, leaving the changeless self, the self being that true part of the complex which is at one with the principle of consciousness. This statement is made from a standpoint that is still relative, in order to show the way, for we do not and indeed we cannot change our nature. There has never been an incarnation: to realize this ultimate truth, we have only to recognize what had hitherto escaped our notice. Therein lies the beauty and the efficacity of the Vedantic method.

---

1. See V, The Relation between Brain, Sense-Organs and the Outer World. "I define reality as that which transcends change." Reality may also be defined as that whose existence can never be doubted (see XXVI, Direct Knowledge), and as that whose being depends on no other principle.

The Restitution of the Self

The non-dual nature of the self is unalterable. Nevertheless, it appears as the witness of thoughts whenever thoughts appear.[2] Identification of the self and the body coincides with the notion, *I am the thinker* (XIX, Thought). But since I can remember having thought, it stands to reason that I am the witnessing consciousness before which all objective experience, including the notion that I am the thinker, comes and goes (XXII, The Thinker an Object of Consciousness). When this is well understood, identification ceases.

Now although identification with the body ceases, the I-thought, so long as a body appears, will continue to spring up as an integral part of the body-idea, that is to say, my brain will continue automatically to present me with the notion that I am the agent, the perceiver, or the enjoyer. But knowing that I am in reality the non-dual self, I shall no longer be affected by the vicissitudes of the body, nor will the apparent duality of subject and object lure me away from my true centre. Egoism has become an empty form; and life, in all its variety, a game to be played according to its own rules.

The Gist of the Method

We have just seen how the adoption of the witness's standpoint prevents identification. But this method has a further consequence. It is impossible to pay attention both to consciousness and to its object: attention, no matter how much it may vacillate, has never more than a single object at any given moment. When I attend to an object, that object alone is present (XX, Subject and Object). But sooner or later,

---

2. See XIX, The Different Aspects of Thought, for the definition of "thought."

I shall think that the object was present to *me*. This implies that I too was present as the witness, although it is the ego that wrongly claims to have been present. If then I pay attention to myself, that is to say, if I see myself as the witnessing consciousness before which the object appeared, consciousness alone is apprehended, not however, as the witness, for there is then no object to be witnessed, but as the non-dual self. This is the highest type of introversive, or subjective, thought mentioned in Chapter IV. With diligence and understanding, the adoption of the witness's standpoint will enable us not only to overcome the erroneous habit of identification: it will enable us to realize, once and for all, that our true self rests in non-duality.

The Superiority of This Method

If our inner and outer senses could be so restrained as to prevent the appearance of objects, it is possible that identification with the body, itself a sensory object, could be arrested. The attempt would not be made, however, excepting by one who ascribed reality to appearances as such:[3] but this we cannot now do. The sole practical means that is available to us for putting an end to identification consists certainly in adopting the standpoint of witnessing consciousness, according to the principles set forth above. When this is done, the senses, which serve only to implement desire, can no longer delude us.[4]

---

3. All those who wish to renounce an unexplained world are covered by this description.

4. Let me caution anyone who may be tempted to find in these words an excuse for abandon: he has not grasped their meaning. They express an important fact, which will be further discussed in Ch. XXIX, especially in Realization and Renunciation.

In short, the knowledge that circumstances affect the body and not the self gives absolute freedom to him who has attained it. Knowing that he never was born, he cannot fear the body's death. He is fearless.[5]

An Injunction Regarding the Personal Application of the Method

I would strongly emphasize that no one should attempt to apply these principles by himself: the method is different in each individual case. Personal guidance from one who has fully realized non-duality is therefore essential. Neither this nor any other book can take its place. My aim here is to indicate a practical possibility which a few happy members of the human species must always have known and experienced. The same warning has already been given (XVI, note 3): I make no apology for the repetition, for this is a matter of supreme importance.

---

5. Here also there must be no misunderstanding: this is not a school for hotheads! I do not refer to animal or mental fear, without which no individual as such could exist even for a moment, but to a supreme and wholly private certitude, which may or may not be reflected in a sage's behavior. Moreover, it will be seen from Part Four of this book that fear is simply the negative aspect of self-love.

–XXIV–

The Verbal Expression of Non-Duality

I remarked in a previous chapter (XVI, Sleep and Non-Duality) that although non-duality abides as the substratum and the reality of dualistic experience, we cannot be aware of it when our attention is turned outwards. It may then be asked how one can speak of non-duality so as to convey its meaning to others; for in order to speak or even to conceive of it, we must, as in fact we unwittingly do, become merged in it, just as in order to "remember" a dream, we must re-enter the dream and leave the present waking-state. Between being merged in non-duality and speaking of it as clearly as words allow, there is no causal relation but what may best be described as sheer reciprocity uniting distinct levels: it could in a way be compared to the reflection of a person's mood in his countenance. But this power of conveying the truth, without effort and in perfect harmony with a seeker's aspiration, is not possessed by all those who have cancelled the ego and met the true self. That one alone who by nature is eloquent and loving, has realized non-duality and dismissed the body, who therefore has nothing to gain or lose by teaching, yes, only that rare being is able to talk of reality and so guide others.

–XXV–

The Problem of Relation

Consciousness and the Brain

The relationship between consciousness and the brain is often expressed as the relation of mind to matter, matter having location and mind none.[1] We can ask, for example, *when* but not *where* a thought occurred. *Where did such and such a thought occur?* could only mean, *Where was the body at the time of the thought's occurrence?* Matter, in other words, is spatial and mind as such temporal. But what is mind as such? It is merely a notion based on the remembrance of successive thoughts, each thought being the consciousness of a something conditioned by time and space which as such is purely sensory: and this notion occurs only when there is identification with the material body (XIX, Thought), itself a notion based on the remembrance of innumerable percepts. We need in consequence trouble ourselves no more with the problems of mind and matter. We have only to consider sensory perception, a sensory perception being the apparent combination of subjectivity and objectivity.

The objective side of a sensory perception is an occurrence in the brain. Being as it were material, it is devoid of consciousness. It is unreal, for without consciousness it could not appear (XXII, note 1). The individual's claim to his being the perceiver, though seemingly subjective, pertains also to the objective, unreal side (XX, Subject and Object). What principle

---

1. I have borrowed this definition from R. O. Kapp's earnest essay, Mind, Life and Body (Constable).

is it then that gives reality to sensory perceptions? It can only be the conscious, subjective side, which remains unaffected by the objective: this principle cannot be other than non-dual consciousness. Non-duality and the brain are therefore the ultimate terms for every possible relation. That they are mutually exclusive is evident.

The Brain as the Locus of Objective Experience

Intellection, imagination, cognition, conation, emotion, identification, egoism, association, the retention of sensations, and sensations themselves, are all inextricably related and the several aspects of normal human cerebration, in which the individual and the totality of his objective experience as such are comprised. Everything that can be called the object of consciousness is therefore an occurrence in the brain.

No Direct Interrelation of Percepts

In saying that the different aspects of objective experience are inextricably related, I was referring solely to the complex processes of cerebration. The percepts that result from these processes, such as general and particular notions of sensory objects, of time, space, movement and change, are not directly related amongst themselves: but each percept is directly related to the single consciousness that runs through objective experience like the string through a necklace. When consciousness appears as memory (XXII, Memory and Identification), it is then that percepts seem to be connected amongst themselves. Even so, their apparent connection is in and through consciousness.

The Problem

An individual's objective experience constitutes for him the whole objective domain. If we attempt to fathom this intricacy from its own level, we shall certainly be disappointed, for the requisite detachment will be found wanting. And if we regard it from the standpoint of the conscious self, which is the sole invariable factor in all our experience, objectivity as such will vanish. As already stated (XXIII, The Gist of a Method), when I see myself as the witnessing consciousness before which an object has appeared, I cannot at the same time see the object: consciousness alone will then be apprehended, not, however, as the witness, but as the non-dual self. This is tantamount to saying that the apparent relation between consciousness and its object must always remain unintelligible. To consider the two as distinct but complementary is not to see them truly: and to consider one of them apart from the other is to evade the issue. The problem of their relationship, as it stands, is therefore insoluble.

The Dissolution of the Problem

Although consciousness cannot be cognized as an object, it is spontaneously apprehended as the self and appears, when objectivity seems to appear, as the witness of all that is objective. Therein lies the solution to the problem of relation. The many and various aspects of objective experience occur one at a time, each, or each group, of which, is the present object of a single witnessing consciousness; and the transition from witnessing to non-dual consciousness is immediate and spontaneous, once the standpoint of the witness has been firmly grasped.

We shall spare ourselves an immensity of fruitless speculation if we boldly acknowledge that the ostensible relation between consciousness and the brain is an impossibility; and that the problem as it stands is delusive, like the assumption in which it has its origin, the assumption, namely, that a duality of subject and object really exists.[2] Why any relationship between consciousness and its object is an impossibility will be explained in the following chapter: we shall discover that they are two aspects of an undivided and indivisible reality.

---

2. To call the problem delusive because one of its terms is unreal is not to disparage those who are concerned with explaining all that is explicable about an unreal objectivity and in particular about the complex processes of cerebration. But there must be no confusion of levels. One such confusion is implied, for example, in the commonly held hope that empirical science will eventually explain everything, whereas empirical science has nothing whatsoever to do with considerations of a metaphysical order. Illustration: the chemist who found his neglected wife weeping and hoped to discover the cause by sampling her tears!

–XXVI–

Non-Duality

The Disparity of Consciousness and Objects

The seeming relationship between consciousness and its object must always remain unintelligible, for if we view them as distinct entities, they are found to be wholly disparate; and if we regard the object from the standpoint of consciousness, its objectivity disappears (XXV, The Problem). This difficulty has often tempted shallow or lazy thinkers to reverse the true position. They say, since we cognize the object directly and seem merely to infer the existence of an intangible consciousness, that the former alone is real and the latter a convenient figment. I hope to have made it clear, in the course of this work, that such a stand contradicts the considered evidence; and that consciousness is no more an invention than the luminary whose light makes visible the page before us.[1] All that has been said, or will be, regarding this matter, may be summarized as follows: that unique principle whose existence cannot be doubted, whose being depends on no other, and which is immutable, that alone is to be called real.

The Inadequacy of the Written Word and Metaphysical Realization

No one who reads this work can ignore the inadequacy of language, or of any other mode of expression, as a direct vehicle of metaphysical truth, for metaphysical truth in reality is

---

1. If you see the page, you do not see the luminary; and *vice versa*.

pure experience. I do not mean that this purely private experience of metaphysical truth cannot be communicated at all, as indeed it can through the spoken words, the gestures and the living presence of one who has realized non-duality. I mean that the written word by itself can do no more than help to dissipate the wrong knowledge that beclouds the sun of the true, at least, for one who has not heard the truth from the lips of a sage: it is then no more than a preparation. But at the same time, one who has been blest by such a presence may well derive pleasure from reading authentic books, a pleasure not unlike that which is to be enjoyed on hearing noble music again and again: a fresh aspect may always appear. And in any case, the truth bears repetition.

In this attempt to give my readers a taste of what by nature is indescribable, I have all the time been aware of using words such as consciousness and self in a manner that violates the standards set by common usage, in a manner that may even want consistency. "Consciousness" and "self" normally denote a personal, subjective principle. We have seen, however, that duality is an illusion, for the notions of a subject and an object are each separate events which recur in memory (IV, The Objects of Consciousness). Knower and known are each the objects of an impersonal principle which I have variously called consciousness, the witness, the principle of consciousness, non-dual consciousness and the real self. These terms I have used in order to establish a bridge between individual experience as such and non-duality. No others could so well have served the purpose of this method: and I must assume that my readers have a ready capacity to look beyond the letter to the spirit. Then, what might easily be taken for so many contradictions in terms will become, on the contrary, aids by which the illusion of duality, the bondage that results from identification, and the unthinking use of a language based upon it, may be finally discarded.

Direct Knowledge

In order the better to understand the statement that, although consciousness cannot be known objectively, it is spontaneously apprehended as the self (XXV, The Dissolution of the Problem), let us consider the assertion, *I am*, whose basic meaning cannot be communicated directly by any mode of expression: it is something that all experience. That *I am* I know for certain; and everybody knows that *he is*. Should anyone, however, feel inclined to doubt his being, we may ask him who it is that doubts. His only positive answer must be, *I do*: and this means, *I am conscious of the kind of objective experience called a doubt*, which therefore he transcends. And should he hope to evade the issue by observing that *I do, if I exist*, he will not have succeeded: the subjective personal pronoun singular always reflects the state of unconditioned being that transcends individuality. Thus he who genuinely doubts that *I am* doubts only that he exists as an individual; and doubting is a characteristic of individual experience. He has intuitively guessed that the ego is not an entity but lacks the knowledge which would enable him to see it plainly.

On Expressing the Inexpressible

It is to prepare the reader for what is to follow that the above paragraphs have been written, for I am about to prove in different ways that, while consciousness and objectivity cannot be related as between two distinct entities, they are, in the final analysis, identical. Here also, no words can directly convey the truth that there is only non-duality. Nevertheless, if those who read on will have been enabled, however obscurely, to discern that which had hitherto eluded them, my attempt to express the inexpressible will not have been in vain.

The Seer and the Seen

When I speak of an object, I imply that something is present to me, the conscious subject. When I speak of myself as the conscious subject, I imply that something is perceived. The complementary character of these terms will be clearly brought out if we speak of the knower and the known, or the seer and the seen. This situates them both in duality; and because the one is never found, and cannot even be conceived of, without the other, they must be the two aspects of one original.

Non-Duality

If there were consciousness of something, there must then have been a change in consciousness, which is impossible. But since objectivity appears in consciousness, it cannot in reality be other than consciousness, whose immutable nature allows of no being other than its own. The oneness of consciousness and its seeming object is proven by the fact that before and after the appearance, or the cognition, of an object, that is to say, when there is no objective experience (as in the interval between two thoughts), the object is non-existent. If it had no existence before and will have none afterwards, it must be inexistent in the middle, for the appearance of something out of nothing, and its disappearance into nothing, are impossibilities. By its existence or its non-existence, however, I refer only to its objectivity. As we have seen, when no objective experience occurs, what remains is the principle of consciousness and not the nothingness we postulate from the standpoint of objective experience. Before and after it has appeared as an object, it cannot then be a mere nothing: rather, it is nothing but the principle of consciousness, that is to say, it is absolute existence. And so it must be, even when the illusion of objectivity arises.

Now if consciousness never has an object, it is a word we can no longer take literally, for consciousness without an object transcends duality. It is the quiddity of all appearances, ubiquitous and unique, and we can only call it non-duality or the principle of consciousness. Why non-duality should seem to assume the duality of a knower and a known, and why the impersonal principle of consciousness should seem to become personified as the thinker, are identical problems: they will be examined in the chapter on "Absurd Questions." At present, we are concerned with non-duality, to which we shall now proceed by another approach.

Matter, Mind and Non-Duality

All objective experience as such takes place in the brain and therefore the distinction between matter and mind is unreal: nevertheless, let us for the moment grant their existence on two distinct levels, since that is our relative experience. And then, since we are able to think about material objects, it would appear that matter is cognized by mind. But how can mind cognize matter? Mind could cognize matter only if it ceased to be itself and became material. If such a change of nature were feasible, it could not be said that matter had been cognized by mind. And how, in that case, could it be said that matter had been cognized at all? Even if it be true, from the standpoint of physics (and granting the independent existence of objects), that one piece of matter may be acted upon by another, matter, being devoid of consciousness, cannot form notions such as those of materiality in general and of material objects in particular. Thus matter has never been the object of consciousness and has never existed. What we call matter must therefore be mental; and the distinction between mind and matter is purely verbal.[2]

Further, since material objects are nothing but notions, it would seem, could we still grant the existence of mind as an entity, that notions were the objects of mind. Mind itself, however, is nothing but a notion (XIX, Mental Activity Defined), based on the memory of separate thoughts. And then, can one thought be conscious of another? We have seen that a thought appears to be a real entity only when there is identification with the body (XIX, Thought), whereas it is simply the consciousness of something. Thus to suppose that one thought can cognize another is to suppose that there can be consciousness of the consciousness of something, which is absurd.[3] A new perception, moreover, implies a new thought, or a new thought a new perception; a thought and its object are therefore at one. This object cannot be material, as we saw just now, nor can it be mental, since one thought cannot cognize another. It follows that objectivity is an illusion. But we refer, in speaking of an object, to a modification that occurs in the brain, so that *thought* and *mind* express merely the ostensible relation between consciousness and cerebration. Can this relation exist?

As in the case of mind and matter, the principle of consciousness could be related to the brain, that is to say, to objectivity, only if it ceased to be its non-dual self and became material. This is impossible, for even if it could change its nature and depart from its being the sole reality to become an illusion, it could not at the same time be a conscious principle and its own object, whether we take the object to be real or illusory. Nevertheless, we do have the experience of objectivity;

---

2. The brain itself is also merely a notion pertaining to duality.

3. See, in this connection, XXV, No Direct Interrelation of Percepts.

and since it can only appear in consciousness, it cannot be other than consciousness.

Wave and Water

Just as a wave consists of water, all things objective, no matter how they appear, consist of consciousness.

XXVII

Metaphysical Realization and the Non-Existence of Memory

Metaphysical Realization

While for plain men, the world is unquestionably real, and its appearance, for those who have looked into the nature of sensory perception, is unreal, it remains both real and unreal for one who has dissolved the illusion of a claiming ego and realized non-duality. It is unreal because its appearance depends wholly upon consciousness, and real because it is inseparable from that consciousness and cannot therefore be other than non-dual consciousness itself. The sage, in short, has transcended all opposites.[1]

Succession Never Experienced

We experience duration only in states characterized by the succession of thoughts (XV, Duration and the Notion of Time). But we have found that consciousness and its object are inseparably one (XXVI, Non-Duality). This indeed is the conclusion that springs of itself from the fact that the notions of thinker and thought are separate experiences, which implies that between consciousness and what we call its object, there is no intermediary. We are mistaken, therefore, when we speak of succession and divide the elements of that succession into

---

1. Reality and unreality, knowledge and ignorance, peace and agitation, pleasure and pain, etc.

so many present experiences: the consciousness in which thoughts seem to occur is a single, immutable and non-temporal perpetuity from which these apparently distinct events can in no way be different. Consequently, there is no experience outside non-duality. The illusion of a present time has as its necessary concomitants the recollection of past, and the expectation of future, events, together with the notion of a persistent individual consciousness. In so far as such events are experienced as real, they are reflections of the perenniality I have called the principle of consciousness: but since they are no more than reflections, they are in truth unreal.

The Non-Existence of Memory

As already stated. I can remember only what I have known. Not only do I remember my thoughts; I remember also my having thought. It follows that I, as the thinker or individual, am the object of consciousness: but as the knower of this and of all other objects, it follows that I am consciousness itself. It is in this way, through the appearance of memory, that the presence of an impersonal, witnessing consciousness has been established (XXII, The Thinker an Object of Consciousness).

Coming now to the very highest standpoint, we shall find that no experience can ever really recur. But it should not for a moment be thought that the witness is something to be discarded. Even for one who has realized non-duality, non-duality will continue to appear as the witness whenever objectivity seems to appear. In his case, objectivity will be like a mirage: since he knows it to be an illusion, it cannot deceive him. And for one who has not realized non-duality, the witness provides the sole means of attaining it (XXIII, The Gist of the Method & The Superiority of This Method). The words that follow must therefore be viewed as intended, my intention being to give the reader a taste of non-duality.

The remembrance of a sensory object as such is an impossibility, for the object had no existence apart from the seeing, supposing the object to have been visual. (It makes no difference whether the object be experienced as "physical" or "mental.") Nor is it possible to remember the seeing, for the process of seeing was ended when what we call the knowledge of the object dawned. But what is this knowledge? If it dawns only when the process of knowing has ended, it transcends the sensory domain and must therefore be devoid of attributes. It is non-duality. But non-duality cannot be its own object and cannot then be remembered. It follows that what appears as remembrance in terms of the senses is in reality the spontaneous self-expression of absolute knowledge. And in non-duality, as we shall see in the next chapter on "Absurd Questions," there can be no question why. This is the last word on appearance.

XXVIII

Absurd Questions

The Origin of the World

From time immemorial, people have been speculating about the origin of the world, making inquiries as to the place, the time and the cause of its inception. Even when the problem of origination is not discussed in these terms, the terms used, no matter what they may be, are always reducible to this formulation, since space, time and causality together constitute the world. But these questions are wholly illogical. If the world had its origin at any point in time, time already existed; if it had its origin at any point in space, space already existed; and if it was as the effect of some cause that it came into being, causality already existed. All such questions are therefore absurd. It would have been more profitable had the world's thinkers analyzed the concepts of time, space and causality as we did in previous chapters (XI to XVI), according to the method used by Adwaita Vedanta.

The Origin of Identification

Let us now consider a parallel problem, one which invariably troubles seekers at the beginning of their search. If the self is by nature non-dual, an individual self must be both unreal and impossible. How then does it happen that we believe ourselves to be embodied? Otherwise put, how and why do we identify the self with a body, granting that a body exists? The question implies that before an ego existed as a result of identification, an ego existed in order to identify the self with a body! This question is no less illogical than the others.

The Fundamental Problem

We have found already that the problem of a first cause is insoluble (IX, Insoluble Problems): what I have just said about the origin of the world confirms it. But since questions of this nature are bound to spring up sooner or later, the proper course is to demonstrate their absurdity, in order that the seeker may reject them and so remain free to devote himself with undivided attention to the fundamental problem, "What am I?" Once this has been solved, all lesser problems will also have been solved, not in the form of hypotheses which can always be disputed, but decisively, in terms of the consciousness without which no problem can arise. The nature of objectivity, in other words, will not have been understood until the nature of the subject who thinks he perceives it has been: then objectivity as such, with all its inherent and insoluble problems, will cease to be a tie.

Absurd Prospects

Persons wishing to enlarge their stock of worldly power and knowledge so as to rise in their own esteem, and in the esteem of others, will not find the smallest comfort in such a doctrine. It will suit those to whom the removal of darkness and incertitude alone counts.

PART FOUR

SELF-LOVE

–XXIX–

Desires, Feelings, and the Witness

The Objects of Desire

By an object of desire, I mean anything whatsoever that can in any way satisfy appetence. It may be, for example, a sensory object, a particular chain or conflux of events, the solution to an intellectual problem,[1] or even the urge to realize non-duality. It may equally be the avoidance or the prevention of something that is feared or disliked: it is then called an object of aversion, but that is only the other side of the coin. And both kinds of object may be definable or indefinable.

Peace the Ultimate Object of Every Desire

Whenever we have the notion of an individual existence, there is always something we desire: and desire is attended by agitation. Being cerebral, this agitation prevents what is called peace of mind. But the moment we happen upon something at present desirable, the agitation (or the latent possibility of agitation) subsides and we enjoy tranquility. It follows that peace is the ultimate aim, though not always the apparent object, of every desire.

---

1. It should not be forgotten that the dualism of mind and matter is unreal, excepting from the standpoint of one who is identified with the body.

The Process of Enjoyment

Suppose I experience the medley of sensations and feelings associated with the idea of hunger, suppose also that food is eaten and that this particular want is fulfilled: precisely at that moment, I am without desire. Next follows a feeling of satisfaction. And sooner or later, because of identification with the body, I shall attribute the cause of this feeling to the food.

Now there is no denying that body and senses were gratified: but was I right in thinking that the feeling of satisfaction, as distinct from the sensory pleasure, was caused by what I ate? To make the question general, sometimes before and always after the happy or unhappy issue of a desire,[2] we have various feelings. What, if any, is the relation between these feelings and the desired object?

The Analysis of Feeling

In our examination of dreamless sleep (III, Sleeping Experience, b and c), we saw that its characteristic peace or happiness in no way depends upon the enjoyment of objects, for in dreamless sleep, there is no objective experience and we are merged in non-duality. Whenever we happen upon a desired object, it is the same. Precisely at the moment of its attainment, the agitation (or the potential agitation) caused by desire is stilled, and we are resorbed in the self whose very nature is happiness or peace: and the object vanishes. This immediate apprehension of non-duality becomes manifest just afterwards in the agreeable feelings we experience: they cannot have been caused by the object, for there was no object in that non-dual state. If plain men do not recognize this immediate

---

2. Unless, of course, we are so transported, either with joy or grief, as to "lose consciousness," in which case the desireless state lasts longer than usual, the brain having become temporarily or fatally benumbed.

apprehension of non-duality, it is for the same reason that they do not recognize the interval between two thoughts (III, The Interval between Two Thoughts).

When, on the contrary a desired object has failed to appear, or its appearance has failed to satisfy, we have disagreeable feelings. We have them because desire was not appeased according to custom or promise and the agitation continued, making the direct apprehension of non-duality impossible. It is this want of fulfillment that becomes expressed in grief, anger, frustration and the like.

Feelings and the Witness

Even though feelings may coincide with the actual or probable outcome of a desire, they point to the ever-present, desireless self and not to any object. Feelings are the objects of consciousness and I am their witness. The senses, in accordance with their own laws and my particular temperament, will continue to seek pleasure and avoid pain, so long as the body continues. But knowing myself to be the witness of feelings as of percepts, I shall no longer have any attachment to desire and aversion. I shall be with myself at peace.

Realization and Renunciation

Only when a seeker is endowed with the one-pointed, all-absorbing desire for realization of the ultimate truth can he overcome all obstacles, whatever their nature. Desire and aversion are rightly thought to be at the bottom of every obstacle on the path of spiritual realization. This often leads misguided or intellectually feeble persons into suppressing them. But no attempt to smother desire and aversion by restraining the senses can, by itself, lead to realization. Realization dawns as the result of replacing ignorance with knowledge and not by substituting one mode of living for another.

Nevertheless, most seekers do exercise restraint, each in his own way and spontaneously: the cultivation of sensory and intellectual pleasure will be found to impede the cultivation of metaphysical knowledge. This answers the likely criticism, that what has been said may prove dangerous to aspirants who are weak-minded or immature. The danger consists in the attitude, "I am a conscious principle having nothing in common with the senses: I am their witness, so let them rip!" No one who thought thus would be fit to follow this method which, as already observed, is intended for those mature souls whose exclusive aim is the removal of darkness and incertitude.

Conclusion: The Yearning for Happiness

All want happiness. Happiness is ever-present as the self. Being ignorant of this, plain men seek happiness through objects. Whatever peace they enjoy must depend upon chance, excepting when it comes passively as in slumber. In any case, it cannot endure.

Well-meaning persons, moreover, who have nothing but an inkling of the truth, are often inclined to renounce the world in the hope of finding the unconditioned happiness they aspire to: and they too will never find it lastingly, for so long as they have not renounced the body by ceasing to identify themselves with it, they cannot rise above desire and aversion. Lasting peace is to be found only when desire and aversion have been properly situated, that is to say, when it is known that they pertain to the ego and not to the self. The ego, as we have seen, is the outcome of the mistaken identification of self and body. There can be no irreversible peace until the ego, or I-thought, is seen for what it is, namely, a mere notion, a bad habit, and the object of consciousness. Thus felicity and self-knowledge go hand in hand.

–XXX–

Self-Love

Self-Love the Spring of All Actions

The aim of all human activity is happiness, and happiness is the very nature of the self. Thus all actions are the expression of self-love. This will be obvious in so far as our private activities are concerned: it may not be obvious when we act to help others. The difficulty, if any, is either verbal or conventional: by self-love we refer normally to self-interest, or selfishness, whereas I use the expression to denote our innate desire for lasting peace and happiness. From the standpoint of ethics, the desire to help others is certainly less selfish than the desire to please our own small selves. From the standpoint of truth, both the desire to please ourselves and the desire to help others, even at the cost of personal sacrifice, proceed from a common motive, regardless of the greater or lesser virtue involved. The motive behind both lines of conduct is the prospect of happiness.[1] It follows that self-love is the sole spring of all action, amongst which must be counted voluntary inaction.

---

1. Cf. the popular song: "I want to be happy, But I can't be happy, Till I see you happy too!"

On Helping Others

Anyone who aims at spiritual realization must be prepared to give up all systematic attempts to help others, even at
the risk of being called selfish.[2] To exceed voluntarily the social
and personal responsibilities required by civilized standards of
behavior could only be a dissipation in the case of one whose
goal is the realization of truth. On attaining his end, however,
he cannot but help spontaneously all those with whom he
comes into contact, either socially or spiritually, or both
together, and these two either actively or passively, according
to his temperament.[3] But "there is no definite law as to how a
person should act when he comes down from the state of tran-
scendental existence, for his conduct is directed by the natural
bent of his mind and the forces of his environment."[4] It is, of
course, only from the standpoint of onlookers that such a
being "comes down": from his own, there cannot be any depar-
ture from non-duality.

---

2. See the author's article, "God helps him who helps himself," *Hibbert
Journal*, April 1955.

3. In this connection, I take the liberty of quoting a verse from *The
Pleasaunce of the Self* by the venerable person Sri Atmananda to whom the
author of this work owes everything, translated from the Malayalam by the
late Lewis Thomson and existing only in manuscript: "In my desire to please
others I lost my centre. Having found it again by losing myself in the nectar-
ocean of the Master's grace, I am established in pleasing others. So have I
gained flawless tranquillity." (From the poem, "Recollections of the
Freeman.")

4. Madusudhan Saraswati's "Commentary of the Bhagavad-Gita," quoted
from Mahendranath Sircar's admirable book, *The System of Vedantic Thought
and Culture* (University of Calcutta, 1925).

About the Author

John Levy was a wealthy English mystic, teacher, musician, and artist who was an expert in Asian folk music and hosted a radio program about this subject on the BBC. At one point in his life Levy decided to give away his entire fortune and go to live for a time in India with nothing. Levy spent many years there with his guru, Krishna Menon, assisting him with the English translations of his guru's books *Atma Darshan* and *Atma Niviriti*.

He then brought his knowledge of Advaita Vedanta to the West in an accessible form through his teaching work and the publication of his books. John Levy died in London in 1976.

SENTIENT PUBLICATIONS, LLC publishes books on cultural creativity, experimental education, transformative spirituality, holistic health, new science, and ecology, approached from an integral viewpoint. Our authors are intensely interested in exploring the nature of life from fresh perspectives, addressing life's great questions, and fostering the full expression of the human potential. Sentient Publications' books arise from the spirit of inquiry and the richness of the inherent dialogue between writer and reader.

We are very interested in hearing from our readers. To direct suggestions or comments to us, or to be added to our mailing list, please contact:

SENTIENT PUBLICATIONS, LLC
1113 Spruce Street
Boulder, CO 80302
303.443.2188
contact@sentientpublications.com
www.sentientpublications.com